Plato on the
Unity of the Virtues

Plato on the Unity of the Virtues

A Dialectic Reading

Rod Jenks

LEXINGTON BOOKS
Lanham • Boulder • New York • London

Published by Lexington Books
An imprint of The Rowman & Littlefield Publishing Group, Inc.
4501 Forbes Boulevard, Suite 200, Lanham, Maryland 20706
www.rowman.com

86-90 Paul Street, London EC2A 4NE

Copyright © 2022 by The Rowman & Littlefield Publishing Group, Inc.

All rights reserved. No part of this book may be reproduced in any form or by any electronic or mechanical means, including information storage and retrieval systems, without written permission from the publisher, except by a reviewer who may quote passages in a review.

British Library Cataloguing in Publication Information Available

Library of Congress Cataloging-in-Publication Data

Names: Jenks, Rod, author.
Title: Plato on the unity of the virtues : a dialectic reading / Rod Jenks.
Description: Lanham : Lexington Books, [2021] | Includes bibliographical references and index.
Identifiers: LCCN 2021043316 (print) | LCCN 2021043317 (ebook) | ISBN 9781498592031 (cloth) | ISBN 9781498592055 (paperback) | ISBN 9781498592048 (ebook)
Subjects: LCSH: Plato. | Virtue. | Virtues.
Classification: LCC B398.V57 J46 2021 (print) | LCC B398.V57 (ebook) | DDC 179/.9--dc23
LC record available at https://lccn.loc.gov/2021043316
LC ebook record available at https://lccn.loc.gov/2021043317

Contents

Preface		vii
Introduction		1
1	The *Quality* of the Unity Arguments	13
2	Unity Passages in the *Protagoras*	19
3	The Unity Arguments	27
4	Rival Explanations of Unity	35
5	Other Indications of Ineffability	47
6	Meaning and Express-ability	53
7	Socratic Intellectualism	59
8	Indirect Argument in Plato	71
9	The Importance of Unity	75
Conclusion		81
Notes		85
Bibliography		109
Index Locorum		115
About the Author		119

Preface

I began teaching at the University of Portland in the Fall of 2004. As it turned out, one of my colleagues at the University was Alejandro Santana. Alex received his degree from the University of California, Irvine, and his director, Gerasimos Santas, had helped me get into the philosophy program at the University of California, San Diego. Alex and I both specialized in ancient Greek philosophy, and, moreover, we had each written our dissertations about what Vlastos calls "*the* problem of the Socratic elenchus,"[1] that the premises in Socratic elenchoi seem to float free. Alex approached the problem from an epistemic point of view, while I tackled it from a metaphysical perspective. (*What justifies Socrates' confidence in the auxiliary premises of his elenchoi?* as opposed to *How can the mere consistency of a set of beliefs entail their truth?*) Alex and I were familiar with much of the same secondary literature, and we knew many of the same Plato scholars. We began having fantastic discussions about Socratic philosophy, and we decided eventually to try our hand at a joint venture. We actually drafted a paper on unity and diversity, but it was rejected. In our discussions about the readers' critical remarks, we found that we had radically divergent views about how—and, ultimately, *whether*—to patch it up. Finally, we found that our differences were profound and irreconcilable, and we abandoned the joint project.

This book presents my own resolution of the difficulty of the unity and diversity of the virtues in Plato. While Alex and I do disagree about the resolution of the problem of the one and the many, I probably would not have begun the examination of the unity and diversity of the virtues (with special reference to the *Protagoras*) had it not been for our initial collaboration. I have great respect for Alex, both as a scholar and as person, but, as Aristotle says, the truth must be preferred.[2]

Just as I was beginning to proof the manuscript, I contracted shingles in one of my eyes. This condition, herpes zoster, results in sharp pain, and difficulty in focusing, and, to top things off, it is currently incurable. (Symptoms can be masked with eye drops but the disease cannot be cured.) My editor at Lexington, Jana Hodges-Kluck, has been very kind and understanding under the circumstances, especially with regard to deadlines. I want to thank both her and her kind and able assistant, Sydney Wedbush.

Nick Smith took time from his busy schedule to talk to Alex and me about the unity and diversity of the virtues, and about working collaboratively. I thank both Alejandro Santana and Nicholas Smith for their contributions to this project, and for their suggestions about how to improve it. Any remaining blunders are my own.

Finally and with special warmth and affection, I thank my grandson, Roman Ganchenko, who did the indexing for the manuscript.

Introduction

Plato often leaves considerable gaps in his work, and for many years, I have tried, where I could, to fill in some of these gaps. I have offered an explanation of the arcane mathematics of *Republic* VIII,[1] and a new interpretation of the reincarnation story of the *Meno*.[2] I have suggested a new reading of the fire in the cave in *Republic*.[3] I have offered a new understanding of an argument from the *Theaetetus* that most other scholars have dismissed,[4] one of them labeling the argument "a model demonstration of how *not* to go about criticizing the [Protagorean] thesis."[5] I have suggested a new understanding of the Socratic theory of piety, applying the theory to the logic of Socrates' defense before the jury.[6] I have argued for a new reading of Socrates' anti-Calliclean arguments in the *Gorgias*.[7] I have suggested that attributing a coherence theory of truth to Plato solves what Vlastos calls "the problem of the elenchos,"[8] Socrates' apparent conflation of consistency with truth.[9] I have more recently tackled Plato's use of images, connecting his indirect style of argument to the theory of images he presents in *Sophist*.[10] In several of these pieces, I suggest that Plato deliberately teases us in order to coax or to lure us out of the cave. By leaving gaps and incomplete arguments in his texts, he seeks to force us, his readers, to enter into the dialogue,[11] which, for Plato, *is* philosophy.

Plato will also occasionally have Socrates say the *exact* opposite of what he himself believes, as when he dismisses the detailed contrast between philosophers and mealy-mouthed rhetoricians in the *Theatetetus* as nothing but a "digression" (177b), when, in fact, it is the very heart and soul of his defense of the possibility of expertise against the onslaught of Protagorean subjectivism.[12] And again, he has Socrates dismiss the middle books of *Republic* as a "digression" (543c), when the middle books contain his fully articulated theory of forms. By picturing Socrates labeling a crucial passage a "distraction" or a "digression," Plato seeks to prod us, his readers, to provoke us to recognize the importance of what has been—apparently!—dismissed.

In these strategies, Plato manifests his desire to avoid spoon-feeding us. He attempts to force us to work out resolutions of many of the questions he raises. Sometimes, however, he leaves gaps out of (what he, at any rate, conceives of as) necessity. For example, he is convinced that he cannot give an account of the Form of the Good, because lower things for Plato are explained by higher things.[13] Accidental features are explained in relation to (higher) necessary features, necessary features are explained in relation to (higher) forms, while forms are explained in relation to the (still higher) Form of the Good. Because there is nothing higher than the Form of the Good (it is "beyond Being" [509b], set "like a coping stone above being"[14] [534 e7]), *it follows that* no account of it can be provided. If an account of something can be given only in relation to something higher, then no account can be offered for the highest of things. He also expresses the fear that, for logical reasons, he cannot give an account of giving an account (*Theaetetus* 201 ff.). At *Republic* 533–4, the "synoptic vision" passage, the philosopher, who has been studying closely the forms, is at last granted the vision of the systematically interrelated array of them all, but this is cast not as a *logos* but as an *experience*. It is not something the philosopher can argue for or even articulate; it is something she must be content to *see*. It emerges that sometimes, Plato leaves gaps because he wants to force us to think things through for ourselves—where leaving a gap is optional—and sometimes, he does so because he feels that he is forced to do so—where leaving a gap is (at least as Plato himself conceives of things) necessary. And these goals are not mutually exclusive. He may want us to think about the Form of the Good, even while he despairs of being able to offer an account of it.

At *Laches* 199e, it looks as if courage is or reduces to the whole of virtue. But at *Meno* 73de, when Meno says that justice *is* virtue, Socrates corrects him. There are other virtues besides justice. Roundness is to shape as justice is to virtue. It looks as if the parts, courage and justice, both are and are not identical to the whole. One way several contemporary scholars have sought to escape this difficulty is to say that "virtue" is ambiguous. Thus, if by "virtue," you mean X, then courage is identical to the whole of virtue, but if by "virtue" you mean Y, then it is not. The other way to go here is to scratch your head, and say, "I'll be damned!" I will be arguing that Plato selects the latter response.

I shall be arguing that Plato believes that the unity of the virtues is crucial for us to apprehend, but that the issue of the unity and diversity of the virtues is, in Plato's considered opinion, something that is finally non-discursive. In what way, exactly, the virtues are *both* one *and* many, then, not only cannot be explicitly argued for, but also cannot even be coherently stated. It is finally something that must be "seen," as he writes late in his career.[15] In a manner of speaking, if the Form of the Good is "beyond being," then the unity of the virtues is "beyond discourse." I will defend a reading of the unity passages in the *Protagoras*, supplemented by material from other dialogues, which places the unity of the virtues beyond the scope of the *logos*.

Now, I am painfully aware that this view is likely to offend many scholars. This will occur first of all because there have been other interpretations proposed for the unity-of-the-virtues doctrine of the *Protagoras*. I cover these and I try to show why, in my estimation, they fall short. Beyond those who harbor different interpretations of the doctrine of the unity of the virtues, some scholars will doubtless lodge a protest against *any* interpretation of Plato which represents him as claiming that certain crucial matters are actually ineffable. A critic of my claims about ineffability might ask whether, if we represent Plato as maintaining that the unity of the virtues is real but beyond the scope of the *logos*, a sophist could use the same ploy, maintaining, for instance, that *sophrōsunē is* "doing one's own" (*Charmides* 161–2),[16] but that the way in which this makes sense is "beyond the scope of the logos"? Could such a sophist not claim that restoring weapons to a madman is, after all, just (whereas *Republic* 332a requires that we agree that it is *un*just), but that the way in which it *is* just is ineffable? Could this kind of move not be used quite ubiquitously as a *logos*-inhibitor, an argument-stopper?[17] In (apparently) sanctioning logos-inhibition, then, the claim that some issues are beyond the scope of reason may seem dangerous and philosophically irresponsible.

Yet there are reasons for thinking the issue of unity and diversity among the virtues is unique in this regard. Someone who resists a strong desire—Odysseus lashed to his mast or Priam manifesting quiet courage in the face of overwhelming personal disaster—exhibits an activity of soul not unlike courage (see *Laches* 191de), yet resisting wayward desires manifests temperance. So temperance and courage seem to be intimately tied together—in these cases, they seem even to melt into one another—yet it would surely be a mistake to say that a soldier who throws himself on a live grenade in order to save his comrades thereby exhibits temperance or piety.[18] The virtues in some ways seem to melt into one another, and in other ways, they remain distinct.

We can imagine a case, I hasten to add, where doing something which manifests, on the face of it, justice, also manifests piety. Suppose I am a dishonest fellow, and that I recognize this as a failing on my part. Suppose I borrow $5 from you, then realize that I probably will not pay you back. I realize that I probably will instead claim that the loan never took place. However, I now suffer an attack of anticipatory conscience, and I undertake a vow to a god that this time, I will make good on my debt. When I do in fact pay back what I owe, the action manifests piety. (It also manifests justice.) But in the ordinary case, when no such vows to the gods are involved, if I pay back a debt I have incurred, the action manifests justice but not piety. It is not thereby an impious act, of course; it is just that, in the ordinary case, piety does not suggest itself one way or the other. At one point in the *Protagoras*, Socrates prods the sophist, asking, since Protagoras believes that the virtues are not one, does he think the virtues are entirely separate?[19] Protagoras answers, "Not that, but not the way you think, either" (331e). Courage and temperance seem to be inseparable, related but different, unified but not just the same—in short, not this, but not that, either.

It is true that it is Protagoras, not Socrates, who seeks out the middle ground between "entirely separate" and "identical,"[20] but there is no good reason to think that Socrates has a monopoly on truth, or that Plato thinks he does. In *Republic*, Socrates thinks he has finished off Thrasymachus (357a), but Glaucon and Adeimantus drag him back into the struggle, suggesting that Thrasymachus has been "charmed" by Socrates (358b). Socrates thinks he is done, but he isn't. Again, it is Protagoras, not Socrates, who says that wisdom is the greatest of the parts of virtue (330a). Characters other than Socrates can make useful observations, and, indeed, as in the case from *Republic* II, Socrates is sometimes wrong.

And again, in *Republic*, Plato seems anxious to distinguish between temperance and justice (*Republic* 432a–433a).[21] Yet if he really did maintain the strict identity thesis which some scholars, notably Penner, attribute to him, he would surely have said, "The definitions of justice and temperance are indistinguishable one from another because justice is strictly identical to temperance."[22] Instead, he admits that the definitions of the two terms are closely related, but insists that the two virtues are subtly different. There are, in short, reasons for highlighting both unity and diversity among the virtues, and these reasons, I am confident Plato thinks, are drawn from contemplation of the natures of the individual virtues themselves. We can see that temperance is *like* courage by carefully examining temperance itself and courage itself. This makes unity and diversity a case unlike justice and the restoration of weapons. In that case, we *intuit* that the restoration of weapons to a madman would not be right, and this because it would be irresponsible. The claim that it would be right but in a way that cannot be expressed is, then, *counter intuitive*. The dishonest sophist we imagined a moment ago, the one who invokes ineffability to avoid refutation, need not detain us here, since we have a reasons independent of Polemarchus' definition of "justice" for thinking that returning a madman's weapons would not be right—*viz.*, our intuitions about responsible and irresponsible behavior.

Finally, concerning certain matters, Plato occasionally waxes mystical. I will cover several other texts where he countenances ineffability. If we do indeed understand why Plato thinks he cannot offer an account of the Form of the Good, or give an account of giving an account, or speak the truth about truth, since theoretical room can be made in these cases for allowing there to be dark corners on Plato's canvas, the claim that the unity and diversity of the virtues is another such non-illuminable matter will perhaps not draw such a virulent reaction among analytically-inclined scholars.

Altogether, then,

1. There are, in the nature of the case, reasons for construing the virtues as unified, or at least intimately interconnected, reasons Plato takes considerable pains to expose.
2. Plato allows elsewhere that some issues are beyond the scope of the *logos*, beyond the scope of rational argument.
3. The view that Plato thinks the unity of the virtues is ineffable accounts both for the inconclusiveness of the unity arguments in the *Protagoras* and for their complete abandonment thereafter.[23]

Now then, as to *why* Plato argues in this indirect way: In his *Tractatus*, Wittgenstein cautions us against transcendence. There are things we long to say which cannot be said.[24] One example he provides early on concerns *facts*. He argues that there could not be a fact about all the facts, because, if there were, it would have to be *outside* the class of all the facts (in order to have all the facts as its *object*), but it would also have to be *inside* the class of all the facts, because it would *be* a fact. Nothing can be both inside and outside a coherently-described class, and so there cannot be a fact about all the facts.[25] With characteristic aplomb, Wittgenstein announces, "This disposes of Russell's paradox."[26] He says no more in this regard, but I take it that what he is thinking is that, just as there cannot be a fact about all facts, so there cannot be a set of all sets. Still, we have a kind of *longing* to say what cannot be said.[27] Wittgenstein specifically cautions us against our proclivity to try to say what cannot be said, our desire to express the ineffable, writing that "what we cannot speak about, we must pass over in silence."[28]

Now, Wittgenstein's cautionary remarks about our desire to express the ineffable are a consequence of his early view of language (that it is strictly a fact-stating mechanism), and others, it is true, have cautioned us against trying to express the ineffable, but they have done so without so comprehensive or explicit a philosophy of language. Lao Tzu tells us that "the Tao that can be spoken is not the genuine Tao,"[29] the idea being that the Tao cannot be limited or compartmentalized, as it would have to be if it could properly be named, designated or expressed. And the Buddha also suggests the crucial role of the ineffable. When he is about to deliver his own equivalent of the Sermon on the Mount, the summary of all his teaching, the Buddha instead holds up a flower and smiles. He says nothing at all.[30] The very center of Buddhism is silence.

The idea that there may be things beyond the limit of language needs to be sharply contrasted with the commonplace that there is truth beyond the limit of knowledge. Stephen Hawking appeared several years ago on a talk show, and said that, in his estimation, Unified Field Theory is just beyond current human cognitive capacity. But, he continued, the truth exists and awaits our becoming smart enough to articulate it. He advised patience: Wait a few hundred years until the human brain has had a chance to evolve some more, and the theory will become available. The claim that there are things that we are not currently *smart enough* to articulate is a very different matter from the claim that there are things which, by their very nature, defy coherent expression.

There also are also truths to which our *current* conceptual system blinds us, but if we should acquire a new system, these will become accessible. Russell advises that we need to supplant our stodgy, Newtonian conceptions of space and time with the new concept of space-time. Otherwise, he warns, we will never understand Relativity.[31] Again, St. Paul says of the Incarnation, "Now we see as through a glass darkly, but later, face to face"[32] This suggests that there are truths that the human conceptual system cannot accommodate. When we acquire heavenly concepts, what now seems obscure and difficult will become clear. And St. Augustine advises *Crede, ut intelligas*: "Believe [now] in order that you might understand [later]."[33]

However, there might be a "heavenly language," or a heavenly system of concepts, which would permit the full articulation of matters which are, owing to our poor, human set of concepts, *currently* beyond our reach, and unity and diversity among the virtues might be such an issue. St. Paul assures us that, although we do not currently understand divine things, "later, we will see face to face."[34] It might be that the gods have access to concepts that we do not. Surely Plato would say that the poets, who blunder about saying (quite possibly) divine things that they do not understand (*Apology* 21b), are *unlike* the gods. Respecting the gods would seem to require us *not* to call them ignorant. (To suggest otherwise would surely be impious.[35]) Either, then, the gods have access to a super system of concepts and can understand what we cannot, or the gods have the same system of concepts we do (otherwise, how could they communicate with us?), and in that case, not even the gods can understand how the virtues are one and many.

As I read Sophocles' play *Antigone*, we are warned against getting locked into unnecessary either-or choices. In that play, Creon takes the ridiculous position that the state is everything and the family is nothing. He even says at one point, "The state *is* my family" (III, 3). Antigone takes the opposite position, to wit, that the family is everything and the state is nothing. Each of these characters pays a dreadful price for her recalcitrance. Antigone hangs herself in prison to avoid death by starvation, while Creon is left in the end without a family. Everyone in his family dies. All he has left is his state. What alternatives were the two overlooking? Creon could have ordered that those killed in the rebellion be buried in unmarked graves. This would have indicated official disapproval of rebellion, but without insulting the dead. Or he could have ordered that those killed in the rebellion receive a low-level burial—one without a eulogy, for instance. Instead, he orders that their bodies be left on the ground to be "eaten by the crows" (207).[36] For her part, Antigone could have found a quiet, low-level way to honor her brother's memory. She could have kept a lock of his hair in a special, secret place in her house. Sophocles is telling us, *Don't get locked into stupid, either-or choices when you have other viable options. Getting locked into such either-or choices has tragic consequences.*

Now, Protagoras makes his not-inconsiderable income by teaching, and, unlike Gorgias,[37] Protagoras offers to teach *whatever* the student needs to know. Just pay his fee, and he will teach your son manners if he is discourteous, courage if he is a coward, stewardship if he is a spendthrift, and so on. What needs to be learned in these different cases, and what Protagoras offers to teach, is, so Protagoras presupposes, separate and compartmentalize-able.

Socrates wants to argue against this view, and there are two ways he could go. 1) He could argue that the virtues are intimately connected one to another. If you alter one virtue, you thereby alter the others also. In this case, there is no such thing as *just teaching courage*. The coward has a whole lot of disorder in his soul, and that disorder needs to be addressed. 2) He could argue that the virtues are identical one to another. You cannot teach someone piety alone, because piety is justice and justice is temperance, and so forth. "Piety alone" does not exist. When Socrates fails to secure Protagoras' consent to strict identity, he falls back on close connection. This comes to a head when Socrates prods the sophist, asking whether, since Protagoras believes that the virtues are not one, he thinks the virtues are entirely separate.[38]

Protagoras answers, "Not that, but not the way you think, either" (331e). What alternative is alluded to here? What lies between "completely independent" and "strictly identical"? Clearly, what lies between the two is "closely, intimately connected, necessarily connected, but still not strictly identical." The arguments that seek to establish strict identity are, most scholars concede, fallacious, while the arguments with more modest conclusions, conclusions like "Temperance is wisdom, in whole or in part, or at least it is *like* wisdom," seem more persuasive. Plato may be thinking here that Protagoras and Socrates have staked out extreme, unreasonable positions, not unlike Antigone and Creon.

Additionally, it might be that *the gods* have a superior set of concepts that they use to understand things that are beyond us. Yet if this is so, when Chairephon asks whether anyone is wiser than Socrates, why does the oracle not answer, "It all depends on what you mean by *wiser*"? Instead, the oracle answers resolutely, "No." In order for the answer to be *responsive* to the question posed, it would seem, the gods must speak our language. But Plato *does* wax mystical sometimes, as when he maintains that certain musical harmonies and rhythms are (mysteriously) conducive to the development of virtue (*Republic* 399ac), and it could be that some concepts we *think* we understand have a divine dimension to them that we do not currently understand. I will return to the issue of the possibility or impossibility of such a divine language in due time.

In this monograph, I will try to show that Plato thinks that the unity of the virtues is ineffable in *our* language, at any rate. Whether that ineffability is a matter of our current woeful state of ignorance (but we may hope for an amelioration of this sad state as we become wiser[39]), or whether the explanation for the ineffability of the unity of the virtues is in the nature of that unity itself is an issue about which Plato, as I read him, does not take an explicit stand. The extreme case would be that not even the gods can account for the unity of the virtues,[40] and I think there is reason for attributing this thesis to Plato. In either case, when we confront what we cannot seem *directly* to express, we typically resort to analogies (the coping stone, the sun, etc.) and stories. Ramsey reportedly asked Wittgenstein concerning what cannot be said, "Can we at least *whistle* it?"[41] Our hunger to see what lies beyond the wall is undeniable.

And, indeed, there is a good reason why we resort to poems and stories when it comes to the ineffable. To argue that something is ineffable would require that we indicate the object of interest (in Lao Tzu's phraseology, that we "name" it), and thus, we would already have designated what we are trying to claim cannot be properly designated. Beyond this, however, we would need to develop a theory about what can be said—and implicitly thereby also a theory about what cannot be said—, and, as Wittgenstein noted, the status of the statement of *that* theory may be jeopardized by the theory itself. If we develop a theory concerning what cannot be said, then the statement of that theory according to that theory (e.g., "Nothing non-verifiable can be meaningfully asserted") may be among the things that cannot be meaningfully asserted.

Wittgenstein himself famously bites the bullet, conceding that the *Tractatus*, on its own terms, is meaningless. The articulation of his theory of meaning would get caught in its own echo. But this unfortunate result might be thought to apply only to the verification principle. Yet consider Popper's amendment to that principle, to the effect that meaning is a matter of falsifiability, not verifiability. The "demarcation" between, for example, astronomy and astrology is that the former has falsifiability-conditions, unlike the latter. No conceivable experience would prompt the astrologer to concede, "The stars do not contain the clockwork of destiny after all." *No unfalsifiable sentence is meaningful*, on this account. But the italicized sentence, if true, is necessarily true, so that everything verifies it and nothing falsifies it. Again, this statement of the theory of meaning appears to be meaningless on its own terms.

And even if an intelligible theory could somehow be developed and articulated which drew a boundary around language and truth but posited an area outside that boundary, early Plato, the philosopher who wrote the *Protagoras*, would certainly be hesitant about maintaining that theory. He represents Socrates telling Critias, "You speak as though I professed to know the answers to my questions, as though I could agree with you if I really wanted to. This is not the way it is. Rather, because of my own ignorance, I am continually investigating in your company *whatever is proposed*" (*Charmides*165bc). He denies sharing "in wisdom concerning things great or small" (*Apology* 21b). At *Gorgias* 509a, he says "What I say is always the same—that I do not know how these things stand," then adds, "no one I have met who tries to state things differently has failed to make himself ridiculous." We are all of us equally ignorant,[42] and it is Socrates' virtue that he recognizes this. It seems unlikely to me that this metaphysically modest fellow would be comfortable making broad claims about the relationship between truth, reality and language. Such a theory might be at the back of his mind (and at the back of early Plato's mind), but I do not think he would feel comfortable positing such a broad metaphysical theory.

Returning, then, to ineffability, either we defend the claim that something is ineffable by articulating a theory of meaning which is in real danger of being meaningless on its own terms, or we use analogies and tell stories which suggest the ineffable without directly naming it, or we pass over the whole matter in silence. The possibilities, then, are these:

1. The ineffable can be named and expressed.
   Or,
2. The ineffable can be named but not expressed.

Or,
3. The ineffable can be expressed but not named.
Or,
4. The ineffable cannot be named or expressed.

1. If we succeed in expressing what it is, then we will have contradicted ourselves in saying "The ineffable cannot be expressed." Indeed, we will have effectively contradicted ourselves in labeling it "the ineffable" to begin with.
2. On the other hand, if we cannot succeed in expressing what it is, then we will only have named it. But some names *fit* the things of which they are the named and some do not, and the only way to be sure that a name appropriately mirrors the kind of thing it names is to check what the name implies against the thing it names. At *Cratylus* 436b, Socrates asks Cratylus, "Do you not see that he who, in his inquiry after [the nature of] things, follows names and closely examines the meaning of each name, runs a great risk of being deceived?" He proceeds to show how a geometer can start with a false premise and construct a flawless demonstration of a false conclusion. But the ineffable is hopelessly obscure, beyond language and beyond thought, so that any comparison between word and object is out of the question. The issue of whether there is an appropriate "fit" between word and object is moot when the object is hopelessly obscure.
3. The ineffable might lend itself to being expressed by poems and stories, for example, but it might still be resistant to being stated. We may be able to approach it by way of gesture or metaphor.
4. The ineffable cannot be expressed, nor can it be reliably named. It cannot even be *whistled*.

I will argue that Plato's doctrine of the unity of the virtues bottoms out in an ineffability claim, and that this claim involves both 3 *and* 4 above. The virtues are unified, Plato thinks, and it is crucial that we should come to *see* that they are profoundly one, but the way in which they are unified yet diverse finally defies coherent articulation. We do not possess a vocabulary rich enough to express how the virtues can be one and yet many.

When Parmenides begins to raise difficulties for young Socrates' (adolescent) theory of forms, difficulties concerned with the relation between forms and particulars, Socrates seeks to avoid the problems by observing that everybody knows there are problems with particulars.[43] He cannot avoid the problem in this way; according to *Republic* 596, we posit forms to begin with because we note similarities among particulars that are properly called by the same name. Many people are properly called "courageous," and so we posit a form of courage that they share.

There is a sense, to be sure, in which particular individuals are not properly called "courageous," at least not *courageous tout court,* just as there is a sense in which particular things may, like Helen of Troy, be beautiful from a certain point of view, but ugly from another point of view. Helen is ugly compared to a goddess, and also ugly because her kidnapping smells suspiciously like an elopement, as a result of which she emerges as a traitor. So, she is physically beautiful but morally ugly. The form of beauty, by contrast, is "beautiful to all and always" (*Hippias Major* 289ac). Particular things are, we might say, "sort of beautiful," while beauty itself is "beautiful to all and always." Self-predication comes to this: What is beautiful to all and always—is beautiful! Yet that Helen and other particulars are beautiful is what leads us to posit a form of beauty to begin with (*Republic* 596a). We must allow particular beautiful things to be beautiful, bearing mind the limitation on particulars that we have noted.[44]

Plato cannot very well say here in the *Protagoras,* "The virtues are one and they are many. Oh well. Everybody knows there are problems with the one and the many." He cannot very well say this because *the one v. the many* is crucial both to Socrates' ethics and to Plato's metaphysics. The unity of the virtues is like the unity of parts of a face, and it is like the "unity" of a chunk of gold, but the unity of the virtues is also, as we shall see shortly, unlike these things. It is finally unlike these things; it is finally something we must be content to *experience.* Plato thinks, as I will try to show, that that unity is beyond the reach of the *logos.* This is why, in his sustained discussion of unity, Plato suggests two contrary analogies, neither of which is even remotely adequate. I will argue that the long interlude on Simonides' "Song" criticizing Pitacus, which other scholars take to be tongue-in-cheek, nothing more than a sustained Platonic *sneer* at sophistic exegesis of poetry,[45] instead suggests a place in serious philosophy for "poems and songs, pipings and dancing and harping" (348a), precisely *because* some matters are beyond the reach of the *logos.* I observe that the individual virtues, wisdom, courage, temperance and justice, are defined in *Republic* IV, but "virtue" itself is not properly defined *anywhere in the corpus,* because a proper definition would have to make clear how virtue can be one and many. If, as I claim, Plato believes we do not have the conceptual wherewithal to express this essential feature of virtue, this explains why he never offers a definition of "virtue."

As to the claim that Plato never does offer a definition of "virtue," it might be objected that he does exactly this at *Laches* 198–99, where he observes that Nicias' amended definition of "courage"—that it is knowledge of past, present and future goods and evils—provides us with something that is true of "virtue entire" (199e). But Socrates does not claim that knowledge of all goods and evils is *the definition* of "virtue;"[46] he only points out that it is true that virtue *involves* such knowledge. Similarly, it is true that virtue is beneficial to the virtuous person, but "what is beneficial to the virtuous person" does not *define* "virtue." Socrates' modest point is that Nicias' definition of "courage" is too broad. Socrates does not offer "knowledge of good and bad" as a definition of "virtue."[47]

Moreover, most scholars see *Meno* as transitional and *Laches* as early. Now, once "justice" has been defined in *Republic*,[48] one does not find Socrates *in later dialogues* bemoaning his lack of understanding about the nature of justice. That question, apparently, has already been resolved. If Plato intends the *Laches'* "knowledge of good and evil" as a serious definition of "virtue in general," why then does one find Socrates at *Meno* 71b saying he has "no knowledge whatsoever" about the nature of virtue? Wouldn't that question already have been resolved, if, indeed, the *Laches* passage is intended as a definition of "virtue"? Has Plato's Socrates *forgotten* that he has already defined "virtue"? Or—is the formula we find in the *Laches* (knowing good and bad) not offered as a definition of "virtue"?

. . . The virtues are one and they are many. *How this can be so?* is a question Plato raises early on in his career, but he is still uncertain about it at the tail end of his career. Vlastos says that Plato wishes to express his "honest perplexity" about how Socrates can hope to find the truth by interviewing hopelessly confused people like Euthyphro and Meno and Callicles.[49] I believe, and I will try to argue, so far as I am able, that Plato wishes, in the *Protagoras* and, as we shall see, elsewhere also, to express his "honest perplexity" about unity and diversity among the virtues.

Chapter One

The *Quality* of the Unity Arguments
How the Issue is Generated

The Simonides passage suggests that we employ a flexibility in interpreting Plato's unity texts similar to what Socrates employs in interpreting Simonides' ode. Hippocrates and Socrates approach Protagoras, who is staying at Callias' house. Socrates asks Protagoras what Hippocrates can expect to get out of studying with him. Protagoras gives two different answers: (1) Hippocrates will get better and better; and (2) he will be taught sound deliberation and thereby, he will be made into a good citizen. Socrates answers that he is uncertain whether good citizenship can be taught, and he asks Protagoras to convince him on this score. Protagoras then gives a lengthy speech in reply. The center of that speech is Protagoras' story about Prometheus and Hephaestus. This narrative contains the detail that Prometheus distributed practical wisdom and fire to the human race but did not initially distribute political wisdom. As a result, human beings could not get along together. Seeing the helplessness of human beings, Zeus ordered Hermes to distribute justice and a sense of shame. The human race was given practical wisdom, but initially, anyhow, the human race was not given political wisdom or justice, and, on this hypothesis, one could possess practical wisdom without possessing justice. Thus, Protagoras conceives of practical wisdom, political wisdom and justice as separable, independent of one another. Evidently, Protagoras thinks that the virtues can be possessed independently of one another.

Yet this story seems to be at odds with what he argues later in his speech. To argue that virtue is teachable, Protagoras asks, "Does there not exist *one thing* which all citizens must have for there to be a city?" He answers,

> Here and nowhere else lies the solution to your problem. For if *such a thing exists*, and *this thing* is not the art of the carpenter, the blacksmith, or the potter, but justice, and temperance, and piety, what *I may collectively term the virtue of*

man [sic], and if this is *the thing* which everyone should share in and with which every man should act whenever he wants to learn anything or do anything, but should not act without it, and if we should instruct and punish those who do not share in it, man, woman, and child, until after their punishment makes them better, and should exile from their cities or execute whoever does not respond to punishment and instruction; if this is the case, if such is *the nature of this thing*, and good men give their sons an education in everything but this, then we have to be amazed at how strangely our good men behave. For we have shown that they regard this *thing* as teachable both in private and public life (324e–325b).[1]

According to this speech, Protagoras thinks that the virtues are one. (It should be noted that his conclusion is relativized, however: Protagoras claims to have shown that the Athenians demonstrate by their behavior that they *regard* virtue as teachable, rather than to have shown that virtue *is* teachable.) The apparent contradiction between the view that the virtues are separable and independent and the view that the virtues are one motivates Socrates' question about the unity and the diversity of virtue: Is virtue a single quality and are the virtues its parts, or are the names of the parts of virtue names for a single thing (329d), as "Istanbul" and "Constantinople" are different names for one and the same city.[2]

A PRELIMINARY LOOK AT THE UNITY ARGUMENTS

Not only is the unity thesis apparently impossible to express, but also Socrates' unity thesis is supported in the *Protagoras* by several arguments which are apparently rather weak. Guthrie charges that Socrates "plays with words," and engages in "elementary fallacies." He uses "quibbling arguments."[3] The argument identifying wisdom and courage is "niggling" and "fallacious."[4] The dialogue is a "labyrinth of petty and . . . fallacious arguments," writes Guthrie.[5] The point of these arguments, Guthrie maintains, is that we cannot decide questions about virtue unless and until we define it. Yet an embarrassment for this view is that, because Plato never does define "virtue;"[6] it would follow that *anything* Plato has to say about virtue is going to be a non-starter. Adam writes that "no other dialogue features so many fallacies."[7] Friedlander basically throws his hands in the air. The arguments in the *Protagoras*, he writes, are fallacious owing to "an iridescent irony, hard to grasp."[8] Wakefield argues that the fact that piety is like justice and vice versa does not entail that piety *is* justice.[9] Taylor thinks the arguments are weak because the theory is incoherent. It simply cannot be successfully defended.[10] Allen thinks he sees the motive for Plato using such unpersuasive arguments: he thinks "blatantly and scandalously fallacious" arguments will help to expose Protagoras, who, "although he claims to teach virtue, does not know what virtue is."[11] Frede also takes the low quality of the unity arguments to be a way of exposing Protagoras as a fraud.[12] Other scholars see Plato's use of fallacious arguments as an invitation to his readers to work out the unity of the virtues for themselves.[13]

An example of a weak argument appears where Socrates seems to be arguing that, since every term has a unique contrary,[14] and since the opposite of wisdom is ignorance, if we locate some *other* state that is also the exact opposite of wisdom, it will follow that that other state *is identical to* wisdom. He then observes that whoever is a coward is foolish, and therefore, since the opposite of both cowardice and foolishness is wisdom, courage and wisdom must be the same. It seems plain (to me at least) that the claim that cowardice is foolish indicates a *property* of cowardice, what I am calling a *true predicate* of cowardice, while the claim that courage is wisdom aims to specify the *identity* of courage. Cowards are foolish, but it does not follow that cowardice is identical to foolishness.[15] And moreover, isn't it just obvious that the contrary of *temperance* is *intemperance*?

Now, Plato himself later recognizes the distinctions between the "is" of predication and the "is" of identity in his refutation of Parmenides. Parmenides has argued that there can be no separation of *what is*. If *what is* were separated by what is, it would simply be *what is* throughout—*what is* would not be separated at all. And so, the only thing that could separate *what is* from itself would be *what is not*, but, *what is not* is not, and therefore has no agency. Plato's Eleatic Stranger claims that Being and Difference are not identical. At *Sophist* 255C, the Stranger distinguishes between two ways in which *what is* (*to hon*) is said *to be*—viz., sometimes, things are said *to be kath' auta* (to be what they are by themselves), and sometimes, things are said *to be pros alla* (to be what they are in relation to others). Difference is said *to be* only in relation to something else, while Being is said *to be* both in relation to something else and in relation to itself. If I break a stick in two pieces, what separates the two pieces is *what is not stick*, but what separates the two pieces is not *what is not* (taken existentially). What is (stick) is separated by what is not (stick). Either, then, Plato later becomes aware of a distinction that had eluded him earlier, or Plato has some dialectic point in providing Socrates in the *Protagoras* with an obviously fallacious argument. Guthrie observes that Plato himself recognizes that some things are neither just nor unjust at *Gorgias* 467e,[16] and this lends credence to my claim that Plato has a dialectic point in allowing Socrates to ignore this in the *Protagoras*, as he here maintains that piety is either pious or impious. Frede explains self-predication by observing that often in Attic Greek, an abstract quality (justice) will occasionally be referred to by the definite article and the adjective (*the just*). It may seem obvious to Plato that, as the hot is hot, so the just is just. What else would the just be, if not just?[17] I will take up these difficulties below, in my discussion of true predication and identity, and again, in my discussion of self-predication.[18]

What *does* emerge from this argument is that foolishness is a *true predicate* of cowardice, but not that foolishness *is* cowardice, where "is" is understood to indicate identity. To illustrate the point, consider the proposition that intemperance is imprudent. What this comes to is that it is contrary one's own best interest to be out of control. But this just means that *imprudence* is a *true predicate* of intemperance. It does not entail that intemperance = imprudence. The claim that "imprudence" is a true predicate of "intemperance" is perhaps what Vlastos had in mind in maintaining that what Plato is aiming to articulate is that the person who is intemperate is thereby imprudent.[19] To say that intemperance is imprudent, then, is both to attribute a property to the abstract entity of intemperance *and* it is to say that an intemperate person behaves in ways that are contrary to her own best interest.

And Plato himself is well aware of the difference between the "is" of identity and the "is" of true predication. When Thrasymachus defines "justice" as "the advantage of the stronger," Socrates says, "Well, it is something advantageous. But you add 'of the stronger.' It is this that I am not so sure about" (*Republic* 339b). Justice, then, is advantageous, that is to say, "advantageous" is a true predicate of "justice." But it does not follow that "justice" *just equals* "advantageous." It appears, then, that it is by misconstruing the "is" of true predication as the "is" of identity that Socrates manages to identify foolishness with cowardice, and thereby, to identify wisdom with courage. The argument identifying wisdom and temperance fails, and Plato, arguably, is aware that it is a non-starter.[20] But it does not follow that temperance and wisdom are wholly separate, either. "Not that, but not the way you think, either" (331e).

When scholars face a Platonic text which seems, on the face of things, ridiculous, they sometimes concede that the argument of that text is a non-starter.[21] Some scholars, convinced that what Plato seems to be saying in the *Protagoras* is absurd, strive to re-interpret what Plato presents, displaying *what Plato really meant*, or *what he should have said*. For instance, in the case of the unity of the virtues, Vlastos maintains that the claim that the "abstract entity," courage, *really is the whole of* the "abstract entity," virtue, would have been "an outrage," sheer "nonsense," and that, consequently, what Plato *really means* is only that people who are courageous are necessarily wise, just and temperate.[22] Other scholars attempt to show that what Plato had to say is right, or mostly right, or at least, right from a certain point of view. Some scholars seem themselves to *endorse* the view they attribute to

Plato.[23] Some transform the view that the virtues are unified to the claim that some single (unnamed) psychological state *causes* virtue, and that the virtues are unified in having that single source or point of origin.[24] Still others distinguish between the claim that the virtues are strictly identical and the claim that the virtues share the same essence, themselves arguing that the latter thesis is true.[25] The unity argument, then, is thorny and there is no consensus on how to understand it.

In particular, the virtues, Woodruff thinks, are one in essence, and that essence is knowledge of good and evil, but the virtues differ in their accidents, in "the things that are true of" them.[26] Suppose I scatter twenty-five ping pong balls on a table, pick up two at random, and ask, "What makes this one different from that one?" The factor that makes the difference is certainly no internal property. The two are identical in terms of all their constitutive properties. What makes one different from another is the *location* of the two—one is over here, and the other is over there. They differ, that is, as to their accidental features. This illustrates what it is for things to be the same but to differ according to their accidents. But I cannot for the life of me bring myself to think that the connection between courage and fear, or between temperance and desire, is accidental.[27]

In the *Protagoras*, we face a series of arguments for the unity of the virtues, which, on the face of things, are not just fallacious but painfully, obviously so. We have only a few apparent options:

1. We can maintain that, appearances to the contrary notwithstanding, the arguments in question really *are* persuasive; or
2. We can hold that Plato was aware that the arguments Socrates presents are non-sequiturs, and that Plato had some dialectic point for including them in the dialogue; or
3. We can concede that Plato, writing a generation before logic had been introduced *as a discipline*, was unaware that these arguments are fallacious.[28]

I think Plato supplies fallacious arguments for the unity claim because he thinks and seeks to show dialectically that logic here has reached a limit. Reason alone cannot take us *near* unity, and language cannot adequately capture it, so, if we are to approach unity at all, we must approach it by way of metaphor. And even the metaphors Plato selects (parts of the face, a lump of gold) turn out to be unsuccessful. I submit that Plato, in striving to express properly his view, has pointedly, deliberately *gestured* toward his thesis, just because he recognizes that the claim that the virtues are one and many, while profoundly and importantly *right*, still evades coherent articulation. Not only can the thesis not be persuasively argued for; it cannot even be coherently articulated. At some point, Wittgenstein remarks, one is tempted just to emit an inarticulate grunt.[29] The one can apparently be many and the many can apparently be one, but in what way this can be we cannot properly articulate.

Chapter Two

Unity Passages in the *Protagoras*

I have already detailed how the discussion arises, but I must recap to highlight a couple of points about the argument. Young Hippocrates and Socrates approach Protagoras, who is staying at Callias' house. Hippocrates is thinking of studying with Protagoras, and Socrates, assuming the role of guardian,[1] asks Protagoras what Hippocrates can expect to obtain from studying with him. Protagoras gives two rather different answers: Hippocrates will get better and better; and he will be taught sound deliberation and thereby, he will be made into a good citizen. These kinds of lessons will not take hold in everyone to whom they are offered, however. Just as some people have tin ears and lack the natural capacity for musicianship, Protagoras asserts, so some children lack the natural capacity for virtue (327ac). This explains why virtuous fathers often fail to raise virtuous sons. But note that Protagoras is fully prepared to take on Hippocrates as a client without enquiring into whether or not he has a natural aptitude for good citizenship, the subject Protagoras claims to teach.[2] Socrates answers that he is uncertain about whether good citizenship can be taught, and he asks Protagoras to convince him on this score. The "wise Athenians,"[3] observes Socrates, apparently think that experts may be consulted about technical matters (319b5–6), but that the common man can be entrusted with decisions about ruling the city, and this suggests that excellence of character is regarded, by the "wise Athenians" at any rate, as a common possession. There is, apparently, no special expertise for excellence of character. Socrates may be speaking ironically here (he hardly thinks the Athenians are wise!), but he does succeed in drawing the sophist Protagoras into a discussion about the nature of virtue as a gauge of whether or not it can be taught. Protagoras then gives a lengthy speech in reply.[4] The center of that speech is Protagoras' story of Prometheus and Epimetheus. The narrative contains the detail that Prometheus distributed practical wisdom and fire to the human race but did not initially distribute political wisdom. As a result, human beings could not get along together. Seeing the helplessness of human beings, Zeus ordered Hermes to distribute justice and a sense of shame. Thus, Protagoras conceives of practical wisdom, political wisdom and justice as separable, independent of one another. According to the myth Protagoras spins, the human race was given practical wisdom, but initially, anyhow, was not given political wisdom or justice, and this shows that, as Protagoras conceives things, one can possess wisdom without justice.[5, 6]

Note that Protagoras also relativizes his claim about the separability of the virtues. He strives to prove that the Athenians demonstrate by their behavior *that they believe* that the virtues are many and separately teachable (324a, 324e), but he does not claim to have shown that the virtues themselves *really are* many and separable. But on the other hand, he refers to his citation of the fact that everybody believes that she has at least *some* measure of goodness as "yet another proof" [*au techmērion* 323a5] that everybody *does*, and this implies that *he* regards his story about Epimetheus and the distribution of wisdom and justice among humans as the *first proof* of the claim that everyone has a share of civic virtue. The claim here at 323a5 is curiously un-relativized. That the claim is un-relativized suggests that Protagoras, for all his posing as a subjectivist, really *does* think his account is true—not just "true for me, here and now" but *true—period*.[7] Not only is his account true (so he thinks) but also, he has proved it true (so he thinks).

Yet this story seems to be at odds with what he argues for later in his speech. Striving to show that virtue is teachable, Protagoras asks, "Does there not exist *one thing* which all citizens must have for there to be a city?" He answers his own question:

> Here and nowhere else lies the solution to your problem. For if *such a thing* exists, and *this thing* is not the art of the carpenter, the blacksmith, or the potter, but justice, and temperance, and piety—what *I may collectively term 'the virtue of man'* [sic]—and if this is *the thing* which everyone should share in and with which every man [sic] should act whenever he wants to learn anything or do anything, but should not act without, and if we should instruct and punish those who do not share in *it*, man, woman, and child, until their punishment makes them better, and should exile from our cities or execute whoever does not respond to punishment and instruction—if this is the case, if such is the nature of *this thing*, and good men give their sons an education in everything but this, then we have to be amazed at how strangely our good men behave. For we have shown that they regard *this thing* as teachable both in private and public life (324e–b).[8]

There is a certain *tension* between Protagoras' view that the virtues are separable and independent and his claim that they are one, and this motivates

Socrates' question about the unity of virtue: Is virtue a single quality and are the individual virtues its parts, or are the names of the parts of virtue names for one single thing (329d)?

The logic of unity is unlike things which have been renamed, argues Frede. He observes that "Istanbul" and "Constantinople" are names for one and the same city, and claims that "courage" and "temperance" are unlike this case. "Istanbul" has a middle eastern ring, but "Constantinople" has a Western, Roman halo surrounding it.[9] *Pace* Frede, however, in point of fact, the history of the name for the city in question is substantially more complicated. Originally, the city was named *Lygos*, a Thracian name (thirteenth century BC). Later, it was renamed *Istanbul*, derivative of the Greek, *eis tēn polin*, "in the city" (tenth century BC). It was again renamed in 667 BC, this time *Byzantium*, after Byzus, an ancient king. Finally, it was named *Constantinople* in 408 AD, after Constantine, the Roman emperor. Both "Istanbul" and "Constantinople" are Western in origin, the first Greek, the second, Roman. Beyond this, however, the two names for the city, "Istanbul" and "Constantinople," do have a different sort of *feel* to them, and it might be said, on Socrates' behalf, that just so, while courage and temperance might *feel* differently when exercised, respectively, by the courageous person and the temperate person, nevertheless, they are each manifestations of a single thing, the *good character*.[10]

Useful though the parallel may be, it, too, is inadequate, I fear. The naming and renaming of a city is an historical matter. If courage (in some way) really is temperance and piety, this is not a matter of naming or renaming. It is not a *verbal* matter at all. Concerning re-naming, compare the case of Constantinople to the case of renaming of Jacob as "Israel" (Genesis 32:28–9 and 35:10) and to the case of the renaming of Simon as "Cephas" or "Peter" (Mark 3,16; Luke 6,14; Matthew 10,2). In the latter two cases, the new name "fits" the character better. Thus, Israel really does *wrestle* with God and Peter, qua confessor, really *is* the rock. But by way of contrast, "Istanbul" does not seem to "fit" the city it names any better than does "Constantinople." "Istanbul" is simply another name for the same thing.

THE GOLD ANALOGY

After Protagoras chooses the alternative that virtue is singular and the virtues are its parts, he claims that wisdom is the "greatest of the parts" [*megiston . . . tōn moriōn*—330a1]. In response to a Socratic challenge, he decides that the parts of virtue are related to the whole of virtue in the way that the parts of a face are related to the whole face.[11] This means that each of the virtues is different from the others, or that the virtues are unlike one another in themselves. Their difference lies in the power or function of each. Just as the nose has a different function from the eyes, so also courage has a different function from temperance. Just as someone may have other functioning sense organs but, like Oedipus at Colonus, have no eyes, so someone may possess all of the other virtues but lack one.

In review, then, Socrates' thesis is that the names for the individual virtues are different names for one single thing, one thing which nevertheless has parts. Socrates presents Protagoras with a choice between two kinds of parts, the parts of a face and the "parts" of a chunk of gold. Protagoras selects the former.[12] The parts of virtue, Socrates seems to suggest, are related to the whole as parts of chunk of gold are related to the whole chunk, or, in other words, that there is no difference, except for size,[13] between parts or between the parts and the whole. One part of the whole of virtue is like or such as (*hoion*—330b7) the other parts. The explanation of their similarity is that the power or function of each part of virtue is the same (*hē autē*–331a7) as the power or function of the other parts. The common functional element of the virtues consists in making possible sensible, prudent behavior in agents (332ab). And this is connected with Socrates' well-known view that virtue alone enables happiness, and that, therefore, no one is deliberately vicious. Socrates *does* recognize differences between temperance and courage, just as he recognizes that there can be differences between chunks of gold. Socrates, it seems, does not take temperance and courage to be strictly identical. However, the differences between virtues are not nearly so stark as to make the virtues unlike each other, as Protagoras had claimed. They are like each other in the most important respect, their power or function. And for this reason, the parts-of-the-face analogy is inadequate.

Now, the claim that the common power of the virtues lies in their regular production of prudent behavior may suggest that "virtue" *can* be defined in relation to that common element. Thus, "wisdom which produces sensible, prudent behavior in relation to what is to be feared" would be the definition of "courage," and "wisdom which produces sensible, prudent behavior in relation to what is desirable" would be the definition of "temperance." Wisdom, so far, appears to be the hub of the virtues.[14] Courage and temperance would be unified in being species of wisdom which produce sensible, prudent behavior, and they would be diverse in the respective spheres in which such behavior is manifested or exercised.[15]

However, justice, unfortunately, does not readily fit the mold. Justice does not seem to be wisdom concerning anything in particular, so it is unlike courage (wisdom about fear) or temperance (wisdom about desire).[16] Justice does not seem to be wisdom producing sensible, prudent behavior in relation to X, where the value of "X" would be something (I know not what!) analogous to fear (courage) or desire (temperance). The "aboutness," the intentionality, seems to be missing with regard to justice. In *Republic*, justice has a special status among the virtues; justice is whole-centered, while the other virtues are part-centered,[17] and so are easily represented as wisdom-about-x. Justice does not seem to be wisdom-about-anything in particular. Now then, a defender of the proposed definition of "virtue" as "what produces sensible, prudent behavior" could seek to drag in ordinary intuitions about justice, maintaining, for example, that justice, as it involves our relations to other people, is wisdom with regard to such relations,[18] but this would be fudging things. We can be unjust to ourselves, so justice is not exclusively concerned with our relations to other people. Socrates certainly *behaves* as if he knows that virtue is beneficial to the virtuous person (see especially *Charmides* 159bc, where he argues that *sophrosunē* cannot be slowness, because slowness is sometimes beneficial and sometimes not, but since it is a virtue, *sophrosunē* is always beneficial), yet he rather strongly denies knowing "anything whatsoever" (*ouden to parapan*—*Meno* 71b) about virtue. This surely is exaggerated, and unjust to Socrates himself. (He knows that virtue is beneficial to the virtuous person.) The claim that Socrates knows nothing at all about virtue is plainly false. If it is possible to be just or unjust to oneself, justice cannot be represented strictly in relation to other people, and Plato arguably knows this. The plot of many early dialogues is a struggle between sophists, who think they know *more* than they in fact know and Socrates,[19] who thinks he knows *less* than he does.

Moreover, if piety is justice concerning the gods (*Euthyphro* 12e), then piety is a part of justice, but this part of justice is concerned with gods, not with other people. Impiety would emerge as being unjust to the gods. Finally, the relevant Greek word, *dikaiosunē*, is closer to "righteousness" than it is to our narrow, legalistic word, "justice."[20] It is what-it-is to live the right kind of human life, in a manner of speaking, the *righteous* life. Justice, *dikaiosunē*, is not only richer than our own narrow, legalistic conception of justice, but it is also richer than the proposed understanding of "justice" as wisdom that produces prudent behavior in relation to other people.

It is true that the courageous, temperate, just person is, *ceteris paribus*, happier than is the intemperate, unjust coward, and for this reason, understanding what makes us happy may seem to *be* virtue. But though virtue arguably *does* make us happy, it does not follow that virtue *reduces to* what makes us happy. Virtue makes us praiseworthy, but it does not follow that virtue reduces to or *can be defined as* whatever makes us praiseworthy. Virtue produces sensible, prudent behavior, but virtue is not just *equal to* "whatever produces sensible, prudent behavior." "Producing sensible, prudent behavior" is a true predicate of "virtue," but it is not, and it is not offered as, a definition of that word.

It may be that Plato selected gold for his analogy, as opposed to iron, for example, because gold is widely known to be *malleable*, and so virtue, that unnamed state of the soul, can be *molded* to fit different situations. A good character, we might say, is manifested in situations of danger as courage and in situations of temptation as temperance. Despite its initial appeal, however, this analogy is inadequate also. First of all, Plato does make reference to the "parts of a lump of gold" (349c), but I cannot see how *a* lump can have *parts*. Insofar as a thing has parts, I should think, it is a composite; insofar as a lump is *a* lump, it has no parts at all. But second, if one divides a single lump of gold into two parts, even if the parts are identical in size and shape (and obviously also, identical in composition), the two parts still will have distinct locations—one will be over here, the other will be over there.[21] It would be absurd to maintain that two lumps broken off from a formerly single lump of gold *are really* the same lump. The two chunks of gold can and do, we imagine, have identical composition, and, we can also suppose that they have identical spatial dimensions, but they will obviously not have identical spatial locations, and it would be required that they have all properties in common if we were to be justified in calling them the same lump.[22]

I think this consideration shows that both the lump-of-gold analogy and the parts-of-the-face analogy are inadequate. Van Gogh was, at the end of his life, without one ear, but he still had a face. But Plato thinks that if you have one virtue, then you have them all, so the possibility of being courageous and foolish does not register for him. (He agrees with Protagoras, who says courage without wisdom is really just madness [*Protagoras* 350c]).[23] What is excluded here is foolishness about what is to be feared. There is still room, I maintain, for non-discursive, behaviorally manifested, bravery.[24] The claim that there is no difference "except for size" between two lumps of gold is obviously false: another difference is their *location*. And though their location is accidental to what they are—*viz.*, lumps of gold—, still, they do differ in this particular, and this shows that they cannot be thought to be the same. And finally, if courage is wisdom about what is genuinely to be feared and (offering a friendly amendment to Plato here),[25] [26] if temperance is wisdom about what is genuinely desirable, then these two virtues do appear to be species of wisdom.[27] But Protagoras says, and Socrates does not oppose him here, that the difference between wisdom and the other virtues is that this "chunk of virtue" is more important than the others (330a). This is inconsistent with the claim that the other virtues are applications of wisdom. Wisdom emerges on this showing as just another virtue, "important" though it may be, alongside temperance and justice, and not as (I think Plato conceives of it) as the *hub* of the virtues.[28]

In relation to the target-phenomenon, virtue, where we (allegedly) have diversity and strict unity obtaining, it is hard for me, at any rate, to see how a (single) lump of gold can be thought to be diverse. If two lumps have different locations, then they are not one single lump. They are two. And if they are one single lump, then they do not have different locations. The location of a lump of anything is an accidental feature of it, accidental, that is, with respect to its composition. But the location of a lump of anything is *not* accidental to it with respect to its identity as an object.

Chapter Three

The Unity Arguments
The Unity of Temperance and Wisdom

At 332a, Socrates secures Protagoras' agreement to the existence of folly (*aphrosunē*) and its direct opposition to wisdom (*sophia*). Socrates then indicates the opposition between temperance and folly (332a–332b). He holds that those who act correctly and beneficially are temperate in so behaving. And those who act incorrectly (who thereby act harmfully to themselves) act foolishly. Those who behave foolishly are non-temperate in so behaving. Hence, the opposite of acting foolishly is acting temperately. Since all terms have unique opposites, and since the opposite of both temperance and wisdom is folly, intemperance is foolishness and so temperance is wisdom.

I have already indicated my own uneasiness about this argument. It seems to me plain that the claim that the intemperate person behaves in a foolish way is not the same as the claim that intemperance *is* folly, in a definitional sense. Borrowing Vlastos' explanation of Pauline predication,[1] I would maintain that St. Paul thinks that love is patient, but not that love = patience. Just so, Socrates would say, intemperance is foolish. But it does not follow that intemperance *is* foolishness. It is only by way of conflating the "is" of predication ("Cowardice is foolish") with the "is" of identity ("Courage is wisdom") that the argument seems persuasive. I have already indicated why I think Plato argues in this slick way.

I have tried to show why, as I see things, the argument from opposites for the unity of temperance and wisdom is weak. That an intemperate person is foolish does not entail that intemperance is folly, nor that intemperance is the exact opposite of wisdom. But Plato also plays a little loose with contraries elsewhere,[2] as in one of the immortality arguments from the *Phaedo*. Here, he argues that, when a thing takes on a quality contrary to the one it had initially, it does so from the state of its opposite quality. If a thing becomes hot, it does so only from a state of being no-so-hot, less hot, or, in a word, from being colder. The argument is set up by a "certain ancient story" (*tis logos pagaios*) about reincarnation. This story is not taken to be gospel truth; instead, the story sets the table for the argument to follow. So, we are encouraged to think, when a thing comes to be dead, it does so from a state of having been alive. This much is obviously true. But Plato then argues that, by parity of reasoning, when a thing comes to be alive, it does so from a state of having been previously dead. Plato apparently thinks that there can be no new life—only resumption of former life. The process of dying thus will issue in its contrary, returning to life (*Phaedo* 69e–72e). Yet if this argument stands, there could never have been creation of the soul. There always would have been living human beings. But *Timeaus* gives us the divine formula for the creation of the soul, so Plato does believe that, at one time, human beings did not exist. I grant that "dead" and "alive" are contraries—that some things are neither dead nor alive, and that, among things eligible to bear the predicates, whatever is dead is not alive, and vice versa. But "dead" and "alive" are not contraries in the way that "hot" and "cold" are contraries. When a new life begins, it does not begin from a state of having already been dead.

At the outset of the argument, having appealed to that "certain ancient story," Plato has Socrates say, "If this argument will not do, some other argument will be needed." He then moves immediately to the argument from opposites. *Here is an argument, and if this will not do, some other argument will be needed. [Then, immediately] And here's another argument.* This shows dramatically that he recognizes the argument from reincarnation is unimpressive. Plato arguably recognizes the weakness of the *Phaedo* argument, so the *Protagoras'* argument about the unity of temperance and wisdom is not the only place in the corpus where Plato's argument from contraries is a little fast.

THE UNITY OF COURAGE AND WISDOM

Protagoras at this point has been worn down to conceding that the other virtues are alike, but he still maintains that "courage is very different from the others" (349d).[3] This is in line with what seems to be an indisputable fact, that soldiers who show courage in battle are typically not terribly reflective persons, and to that extent, not properly wise persons.[4] Soldiers are also not notoriously temperate! This may explain why Plato devotes so much energy to arguing that courage and wisdom are inextricably linked together: we have a strong intuition to the contrary, an intuition which Plato feels he must resist.

Socrates secures Protagoras' agreement that the courageous (*andreia*[5] 350b6) are confident (*tharsaleos* 349e2) and that the courageous are ready for action (*itas* 349e3). It is established in the *akrasia* passage (353 ff.) that failure to be in control of oneself is due to ignorance (*anamathia* 357d3), and that no one pursues things that she believes are genuinely dreadful. Thus, all people, both the courageous and the cowardly, pursue things about which they are confident.

Although courageous people and cowardly people pursue those things about which they are confident, still, they are confident about opposite things. Courageous people are willing to go to war, but cowards are not. But going to war is fine, good, and pleasant. Hence, courageous people pursue what is fine, good and pleasant, and their confidence or fear is correspondingly fine and good. Cowards, on the other hand, pursue what is foul, bad and painful, and their confidence or fear is correspondingly bad and foul. Since cowards pursue what is foul, bad and painful, and since their fear or confidence is also foul and bad, their fear or confidence is due to ignorance of what is truly to be feared and of what is not to be feared. No one pursues what she thinks is dreadful. Thus, ignorance about what is (genuinely) to be feared *is* cowardice.[6] Those who pursue what is shameful do so only because they do not properly know what is honorable and what is shameful. Since the contrary of cowardice is courage, wisdom about what is (genuinely) to be feared and what is not (genuinely) to be feared is courage.

Still, this argument shows, I think, that courage can be represented as a specific kind of wisdom, wisdom about the things that are genuinely dreadful, but it does not show that courage and wisdom are the same. When Laches defines "courage" in strictly military terms at 190E, Socrates points out that one can show courage in non-military situations, when, for example, one resists a very strong temptation. This seems to identify courage with temperance. But though it shows courage and temperance are drawn from the same well, so to speak—both involve the steady, bloody-minded resolve to stick by one's principles, not to be swayed by contrary desires—it just does not follow that courage *is* wisdom. Wisdom, it seems, is the wider of the two phenomena; one can also be wise about what is truly desirable, which manifests temperance.[7] Since we can display wisdom in spheres other than the sphere concerned with what is dreadful, the argument shows that courage *requires* wisdom, but does not show that courage *equals* wisdom.

One small wrinkle should be noted here. Plato has a tendency, here and elsewhere, to run "knowledge" together with "wisdom." But perhaps we should be more careful about the difference. Brave but unreflective soldiers, we might say, do not, properly speaking, have *knowledge* concerning the things that are genuinely dreadful—they would "flunk an elenctic exam," as Vlastos puts it[8]—, but they do manifest wisdom concerning these things.

Their behavior is the natural effluence of their implicit wisdom. This wisdom might be non-discursive. And if it is non-discursive, this would explain why virtue cannot be reliably *taught*. Brave soldiers show *by their behavior* that they understand that some things are worse than death, even though this thought, arguably, never crosses their minds.

THE UNITY OF JUSTICE AND PIETY

The argument that justice and piety are one is brief, and Plato has Protagoras interrupt it (at 332a). He does not revisit the issue in the *Protagoras*. Socrates seems to be arguing that justice is just and that piety is pious. Since justice is not impious, justice must also be pious. Socrates holds that either piety is pious or it is impious. He concludes that, since piety cannot be impious, it must be pious.

The argument clearly requires self-predication. Plato needs the premise that piety is pious. Guthrie maintains that Plato later gets nervous about self-predication, but that he accepts it uncritically here in *Protagoras*.[9] In *Euthydemus*, Plato satirizes the way the sophists present either-or choices (see also *Gorgias* 467e on this same proclivity), but here in *Protagoras*, Socrates seems to engage in that very practice, insisting that either piety is pious or that piety is impious. He concludes that, since piety cannot be impious, it must be pious.[10]

Detour: Self-Predication

Savan believes that, in maintaining self-predication, Socrates means only that the *dunamis* or power of pious people lies in pious action.[11] Still, it does seem outrageous to argue, because the eye has the *dunamis* of sight, that sight *sees*. Vlastos, as already noted, thinks the view that the "abstract entity," piety, has the property of being pious would be an outrage, and so what Plato must mean is only that pious people are pious.[12] As I have already indicated, I think that Plato believes that the fact that a claim conflicts with common sense does little to undermine the claim. Socrates thinks no one does the wrong thing willingly, and that fact that *the Many* reject this thesis does not faze Socrates in the slightest. Indeed, he enlists Protagoras' help in refuting *the Many* on this issue (333c ff.). The fact that almost everyone denies Socrates' thesis, that it is an outrage against common sense, does not appear to disturb Socrates at all.

Self-predication, the apparent claim that beauty itself is beautiful, has caused quite a stir among scholars.[13] The idea that the abstract entity, beauty itself, possesses the quality of beauty has struck many as absurd, while others have sought to explain it away. The issue *does* arise in connection with Socrates' argument about the unity of justice and piety, so I will sketch my own view about that issue here, but only briefly, since the issue really is ancillary to the unity of the virtues, which is my chief stalking horse.

Hippias Major 289de contrasts the form of beauty with a beautiful particular thing. Particular things suffer from aspect-dependence, unlike forms. Consider the myth of Helen and Paris. At the marriage festival of the gods, Envy, who has not been invited, has sent by way of messenger a wreath to be awarded to the fairest of the goddesses. This starts a quarrel about who the fairest of the goddesses is. The choice finally comes down to Aphrodite or Athena, representing, respectively, sexual love or wisdom. The dispute is referred to Zeus, but Zeus refuses to get involved, and suggests that a mortal be appointed to make the decision. Paris, son of Priam, King of Troy, is selected. Each goddess offers Paris a bribe. Athena promises him all the wisdom in the world, but Aphrodite promises him the love of the most beautiful woman in the world, and this is the bribe that is successful. Aphrodite wins. The most beautiful woman in the world is Helen, who is already married to Menelaus. But with the goddess' help, Helen is spirited away. This sets in motion the War between Troy and Achaea.

Now then, Helen of Troy is beautiful in one way—the most beautiful of women is, after all, what Paris was promised by Aphrodite. Yet compared to a goddess, Helen is ugly.[14] And Helen does seem not so much to be a victim of a kidnapping as she does a participant in an elopement. Presumably, then, Helen is ugly *qua* traitor. She is, then, beautiful in one way, but ugly in another way, beautiful from one point of view, ugly from another, and so on. But the form of beauty is "beautiful to all and always" (*Hippias Major* 289b).

Let us take the form of beauty to be *what is beautiful to all and always*. Plugging in this understanding to self-predication, then, *what is beautiful to all and always* is beautiful. That is to say, *what is truly beautiful—is beautiful*! Put in this way, self-predication seems obvious. It seems, indeed, trivially true. It seems, indeed, analytic, to use an old-fashioned term. At *Phaedo* 74bc, Socrates asks, "Has the equal ever seemed unequal to you?" in contrast to equal particulars, which do seem unequal at times. Consider the following:

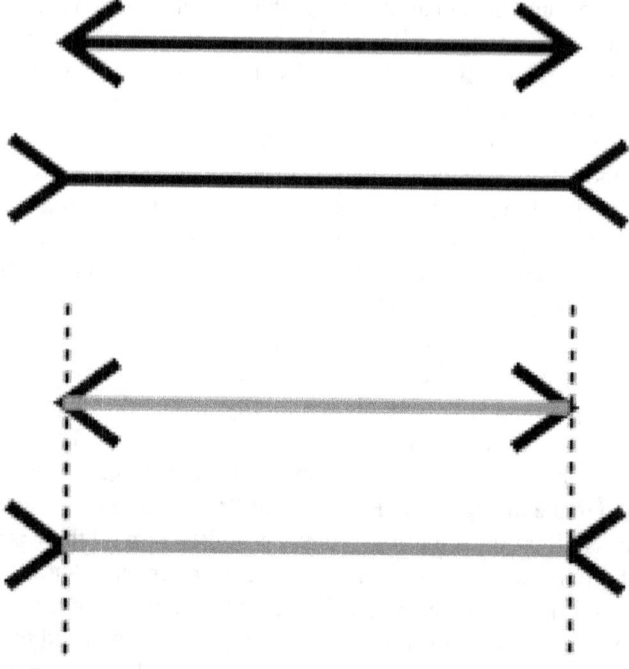

Figure 3.1. Muller Optical Illusion. *Source:* Public Domain

These particular lines segments are equal, but they appear unequal. But equality itself, what-it-is to be equal, what is equal through and through—is equal. Thus, what is equal without qualification—is equal!

Allen makes much of the fact that the expression for equality-what-it-is that Plato uses here is "the equals." So he asks, "Have the equals ever appeared unequal to you?" But I take "the equals" here to come to "what are truly equal," and not to "equal particular things like sticks and stones [and line segments]." Things which really are equal—the line segments above, for instance—may appear to be unequal in certain settings. But equality itself—what is equal through and through—this has never and never will appear unequal. And the answer Socrates receives to his query, "Has the equal ever seemed unequal to you?" is "Never yet at any time!" This shows how obvious self-predication seems to Plato. As it is for equality, so too it is for piety—what is truly pious, pious from all points of view—is pious.[15]

And what is the idea behind the complaint about equality?—If two things are equal, then they had jolly well better appear to be equal at all times? Really? The line segments case features things that are equal but appear not to be so, and this seems to be endemic to particulars. This is why particular things are said to "wander around between being and not-being" (*Republic*

479bc). A particular law may seem just from one point of view and unjust from another, or just for one slice of time but unjust for another—the particular law "wanders around" between justice and injustice—but justice itself is just through and through.

Protagoras accuses Socrates of fallacious reasoning at this point. Socrates has claimed that, because justice is just and because piety is just, that "justice is either the same thing as piety or very like it" (331b). That is, I take it, justice and piety both have "pious" as a true predicate. Protagoras replies that even contraries have some features in common, but it does not follow that contraries are identical.[16] White is like black and hard is like soft, but white ≠ black and hard ≠ soft. Socrates now poses a false dilemma to Protagoras: either he must admit that piety and justice are one, or he must say that "there is only a slight resemblance between them" (331e). Protagoras wants to suggest that they loosen up this disjunction; he does not wish to maintain that the two are identical, nor does he wish to say that they are only slightly similar. In response to Socrates' characterization (that he, Protagoras, believes justice and piety to be only slightly similar), Protagoras replies, "Not quite that, but not in the way you believe, either" (331e–332a). At this point, Socrates drops the argument abruptly, turning instead to wisdom and temperance. I think that Plato at this point may feel a certain sympathy for Protagoras. The virtues are many *and* the virtues are one, and their relationship to one another is not a matter of strict identity nor is it a matter only of a "slight resemblance." It is not exactly one way nor is it exactly the other way.[17] I believe that Plato himself agrees with Protagoras here—the virtues are not exactly identical but they are not exactly separate, either.

The upshot seems to be that maybe justice and piety are one, but that this is not the way to argue that they are. Given that Plato elsewhere recognizes false dilemmas,[18] it seems likely that he at least *senses* that Socrates' argument for the unity of justice and piety is not particularly cogent. This would explain why Socrates abruptly drops the argument for their unity. And Plato's recognition of the weakness of this argument is entirely consonant with my claim that, as he sees things, the virtues (including justice and piety) *are* one, but not in a way that be properly argued for or even clearly stated.

SIMONDES

Turning for a moment to poetry, just as Simonides[19] rebukes Pittacus for having made a false and dangerous claim about being and becoming good, so Socrates sets out to rebuke Protagoras for having made a false and dangerous claim about virtue. Socrates imagines Simonides saying (in effect) to Pittacus,

"If you spoke with even a moderate degree of reasonableness and truth, . . . I would never blame you. But as it is, you have made an utterly false statement about a matter of the highest importance, and it passes for true. For this, I do blame you" (346e–347a). This is exactly Socrates' relation to Protagoras himself. Protagoras, Socrates thinks, has said false and dangerous things (i.e., in particular, relativistic things) about virtue, and this is a matter of the highest importance. Simonides can achieve what he sets out to achieve without articulating a whole theory of the good; Socrates can achieve what *he* sets out to achieve without articulating (that which I maintain he at least *thinks* he *cannot* articulate), a whole theory of virtue. Socrates' looseness in this regard is just what we should expect on the basis of the Simonides passage.

I believe that Plato is peering through the text at the point when Socrates is expounding to Protagoras the real meaning of Simonides' "Ode." It is as if *Plato* as a writer is saying, "Appreciate *the dialogue you are now reading* in relation to its goals. Do not demand too much from it." One of the lines from Simonides that Socrates and Protagoras discuss runs, "I do not seek a blameless man, . . . but should I find him, you will have my report" (346d). Plato might thus continue, "*I* do not have a fully delineated theory of virtue, but if I should develop one, you will have *my* report." I hasten to add that, if I am right that Plato believes that an essential feature of virtue is ineffable, such a fully delineated, fully articulated theory cannot be given, not even by the gods. Unity is, in the end, something we must *experience*.

Chapter Four

Rival Explanations of Unity
Biconditionality as an Explanation of Unity

According to Vlastos, Plato thinks that the virtues are equivalent and related biconditionally, that is, one is courageous if and only if one is wise; one is wise if and only if one is just; one is just if and only if one is temperate; and one is temperate if and only if one is pious. When the biconditionality thesis is applied to people, the individual virtues are "inter-predicable." Vlastos explains this feature of virtue by appealing to what he calls "Pauline predication." St. Paul writes that love is patient and kind, that love is not jealous or proud, etc. (1 Corinthians 13,4). When we say things like "Love is patient," "Justice is impartial," or "Love is blind," we mean that *people* who are just are impartial, that *people* who are love are blind, etc. We do not mean to imply that the "abstract entity," justice itself, is blind. *That* view, Vlastos says flatly, would be "nonsense." Similarly, to claim that courage is the whole of virtue would be "an outrage."[1] Instead, Plato must mean that "courageous" is predicable of virtue, and this amounts to the claim that virtuous people are courageous.

Vlastos' view, however, is problematic. To begin with, the passages cited by Vlastos as evidence against the identity thesis also count as evidence against the equivalency thesis.[2] For example, Vlastos cites the *Euthyphro* (12c–d), where Socrates claims that where there is piety, there is justice, but *not vice versa*, and Vlastos uses this passage to argue that Socrates could not have held the identity view. This same passage, however, can be used to argue against the equivalency or biconditionality thesis, because it shows that, while piety implies justice, justice does not imply piety. Again, Vlastos' view does not adequately account for Plato's view that wisdom is especially crucial for the possession of any of the other virtues.[3] Wisdom is the hub of the virtues; but Vlastos represents it as just another spoke. He also takes Socrates to mean that wisdom is necessary and sufficient for the possession of any other virtue.[4] However, if the virtues are all related biconditionally, then it seems that wisdom is *not* central to the acquisition of the other virtues. Wisdom is just one of the many parts of virtue, and, while it would still be true that wisdom is necessary and sufficient for the possession of any other virtue, the same could be said for piety. But Socrates does seem to think that wisdom is especially crucial for the other virtues.[5] Lastly, any interpretation of Socrates' unity thesis must make sense of Socrates' claim that all of the virtues are at bottom the same. Vlastos dismisses this claim by arguing that it implies the identity view, which he thinks Socrates could not have held because it is an "outrage" against common sense. However, Socrates does not seem to be at all embarrassed about his views being at odds with common sense.[6] When Polus suggests that a vote among the spectators will settle the quarrel between Socrates and himself as to whether or not tyrants have great power, Socrates tells him, "You do not sway me at all by producing all these false witnesses against me" (*Gorgias* 472b). "The truth," he is confident, "is never refuted" (*Gorgias* 473b10), and it certainly is not refuted by the fact that common sense fails to acknowledge it. Additionally, Socrates suggests his alternative claim again (349 ad) upon returning to the topic *after* the Simonides passage.[7] This strongly suggests that in addition to being concerned with the question of whether one could possess a virtue to the exclusion of the others, Socrates is *also* concerned with the question of whether the virtues are indeed the same. Finally, Plato surely intends to convey to his readers that Socrates was courageous (not only the way he behaved at Delium [*Laches* 181b] but also the way he faces his own execution testifies to this), yet Socrates denies knowing what courage is. See especially *Laches* 186de, where he "den[ies] having any knowledge at all of the subject." This strongly suggests that it is possible to have courage-in-character without having courage-wisdom, or having behaviorally manifested rather than theoretical wisdom, and so, while wisdom implies courage, courage does not seem to imply wisdom.[8]

Concerning the *Laches* passage that Vlastos frets about, where courage as understood by Nicias turns out to be the whole of virtue, Penner takes this to be flatly true, but there is available a less radical interpretation. It might be that Socrates thinks that you *cannot understand* a part of virtue (like courage) in isolation from the whole of which it is a part. This, indeed, is the flip side of the view one finds in the *Meno*, where Socrates says that if you understand any one thing, you can infer everything else from it, because "the natures of all things are in kinship" (81d). Just as you cannot understand a spark plug without understanding that it is part of an engine (along with pistons and condensers and what-not), so you cannot understand courage without understanding virtue and the other virtues.[9] The point may have to do with understanding courage, what-it-is—when you try to separate off a virtue like courage and try to understand it all by itself, you are inevitably led back to the whole which you have artificially divided. This, indeed, is (I believe) why, when in *Republic*, we get a definition of "justice," we also get definitions of "wisdom," "courage," and "temperance": justice cannot be understood in isolation from the whole of which it is a part.

Now, as for "knowledge of good and evil" being taken by Vlastos, Brickhouse and Smith and a host of others as a definition of "virtue entire," it should be observed here that *Meno* comes, according to standard chronologies, long after *Laches*. Yet the topic of *Meno* is the nature of virtue. It begins with Meno flinging this question at Socrates: "Tell me if you can Socrates, how virtue is acquired?" (*Meno* 70a). Socrates answers that the prior question is "What is virtue?" and they address that question. If Plato intends "knowledge of good and evil" in the *Laches* to be the definition of "virtue," why does he devote a whole new dialogue to that very question, a dialogue that is written considerably later in his career? Has he *forgotten* that he has already defined "virtue"? The other possibility, the one I opt for, is that "knowledge of good and evil" is a *true predicate* of "virtue," but it is not, and it is not offered as, a definition of that concept.

STRICT IDENTITY AS AN EXPLANATION OF UNITY

According to Penner, the virtues are strictly identical to each other, that is, courage = wisdom = temperance = justice = piety. Virtue-names refer to some unnamed *psychological state* that "explains the fact that certain men [*sic*] do virtuous acts."[10] When Socrates asks what courage is, he is *not* asking for an explanation of what we *mean* by "courage;" he is asking for an explanation of that *psychological state* that makes courageous people courageous. Penner illustrates this as follows: We believe that water is strictly identical with H_2O, yet we are not committed to claiming that "water" and "H_2O" can be substituted one for the other in all contexts.[11] We can speak of "Holy Water," but not we cannot speak, *comfortably* anyhow, of "Holy H_2O," yet nevertheless, all water, even Holy Water, is, strictly speaking, H_2O As Freud tries to discover what hysteria is by seeking its root cause, so, Penner argues, Plato wishes to discover what courage is by seeking *its* root cause. Just as Freud is not making a claim about the meaning of "hysteria," nor is he making a claim about the proper analysis of the concept of hysteria, so too Plato is not making a claim about the meaning of *andreia*, nor is he making a claim about the proper analysis of *that* concept. Penner then reasons that "since the identity conditions for psychological states are presumably *wider* than synonymy, we can suppose that two non-synonymous virtue-words refer to the same psychological state."[12] The different virtue-names can all refer to one and the same psychological state, despite the fact that the same psychological state results in different *behavior* in different contexts. One can grant that courageous behavior is different from pious behavior—and even grant that the virtue-words we use to name courageous and pious acts are non-synonymous—without supposing that each kind of virtuous act requires a different psychological cause. Socrates' unity thesis is thus represented as a strict identity claim.[13]

Perhaps the analogy to Freud deserves some more attention. The real cause of hysteria, Freud thinks, is unconscious wishes, so strong that they demand expression but so difficult for us to acknowledge that their expression is altered to protect us. The Wolfman wishes for anal satisfaction from his father, but his conscious minds cannot handle that realization, so he instead becomes hysterically constipated. Every week, the Wolfman must visit a hospital to receive an enema administered by a male nurse—which is *almost* what he wants. But not quite. In positing this explanation, Freud is not waxing definitional. He is not telling us about the meaning of "hysteria," nor is he telling us about the meaning of this instance of hysteria. He is seeking the root cause, and thus, the explanation, of this instance of hysteria. The wish is the posited psychological cause of the constipation.

Socrates is seeking, Penner urges, the psychological cause of courageous behavior. And Penner's hypothesis is that such behavior is caused by wisdom about what is fearful or dreadful. Socrates, we may say, effectively tells the jury, "You cannot touch my soul. If you could harm my soul, if you could make me unjust, that would be something I would dread. But as it is, you can only harm my body." His facing of his conviction and execution is motivated by his wisdom about what is (and most especially, about *what is not*) truly frightening.

A difficulty for Penner is that one can, apparently, be virtuous by nature. One can be naturally temperate or naturally courageous—without, that is, pursuing the definitions of "temperance" or "courage." See *Charmides* 157–8 on *inherited* temperance.[14] The right kind of wisdom reliably produces virtue, but it is not strictly necessary for virtue.[15] Some children are (evidently) by nature courageous, or at least, bloody-minded, but without the element of wisdom.

I concede that Socrates intends to argue that all the virtues are *in some sense* one and the same. But it is important to take seriously several qualifications that Socrates inserts when he presents his unity thesis. Socrates claims that there is no difference, "except for size," between the virtues and that they are "*most like*" one another. But to say that x is strictly identical to y systematically *precludes* one from adding "*except* in certain respects," or from saying, "At least, x is *most like* y." If x is *unlike* y in some respect, *any* respect, if the two differ *even slightly*, then x is not *strictly identical* to y. If there is *any* discernable difference between x and y, then x ≠ y.[16]

Penner might reply that these passages are preliminary expressions of a *clearer* unity thesis that Socrates expresses later in the dialogue. Or again, he might dismiss these passages as part of an initial skirmish between Socrates and Protagoras that is irrelevant to the unity thesis argued for later in the dialogue. But there does not appear to be a non-question-begging reason for why we should dismiss these passages as irrelevant to the interpretation of Socrates' unity thesis. The "except for size" remark is made *in the middle of* the gold analogy, to which Socrates refers again at 349 a–d, well *after* he has given his first argument that temperance is wisdom. And the claim that the virtues are "most like" each other is made in the middle of his claims that justice is like piety and piety is like justice, and again, Socrates refers *back* to his claims in this passage immediately *after* he argues that temperance is wisdom. Socrates says, "Would not that make wisdom and temperance one thing? And a little while ago it looked as if justice and piety were nearly the same thing." If Socrates here is concluding that wisdom and temperance are one psychological state, then it is odd that he refers to justice and piety as *nearly the same* thing. Socrates does appear to hold that the virtues are at bottom one psychological state, yet his qualifications are enough to give us pause when it comes to construing the claim as one of strict identity.

And when Meno says at *Meno* 73d that justice *is* virtue, Socrates corrects him, holding that justice is to virtue as whiteness is to color and as roundness is to shape. That is, justice is a virtue, but there are other virtues, too. Yet if he really maintained strict identity, he would have agreed with Meno here.

Skepticism About Words: Rorty

In his important book, *Philosophy and the Mirror of Nature*, Rorty argues that philosophy has been confused from the get-go. A philosopher like Socrates who is interested in courage should carefully observe people doing courageous things, and draw her conclusions from that examination. Instead, philosophers routinely study our "conceptual system," or the ordinary use of "courage" and its cognates. While such an examination might yield all kinds of interesting information about our conceptual system and about our language, it does not address its (apparent) target, the nature of courage. Courage is "out there" in the world. That is where we should be looking if we seek to explain what courage is. The "mirror" of nature—the mind, our language—may well have properties of its own, properties which distort what the mirror reflects. The safest thing to do is to look, not to the mirror of nature but rather, to nature itself to locate natural things. Thus Rorty.

And this proposal is connected to Quine's larger project of turning philosophical questions over to the empirical sciences.[17] What we have (mistakenly) taken for *a priori* questions are really just extremely general empirical questions, Quine maintains. Suppose courageous behavior is enabled by psychological state B. Then psychological state B *is* courage. Psychological states are "out there" in the world, and can be studied by the empirical sciences. And courage, "what it is" as Plato puts it, is not to be found by studying the use of words or the logic of concepts in the mind—it is to be found "out there," in the world.

A Rortyan, to coin a phrase, might maintain that certain objections to the strict identity construal of unity rely on the mistake Rorty identifies. *What courage really is* is not revealed by how we use the word "courage" or by what we mean by calling an action "courageous." It is revealed by the empirical sciences.[18] It is thus no objection to the claim that courage is strictly identical to temperance that *we would not say* that a soldier who threw herself on a live grenade to save her buddies acted *temperately*, while we would say that that soldier acted *courageously*. This does not show that courage ≠ temperance, since the claim that courage is strictly identical to temperance is *not* a claim about words, their use(s) or "what we say when." It is a claim about courage *what-it-is*. The identity claim is a type-type claim. The logic of tokens is irrelevant. As water is H_2O, and this fact is not contradicted by the fact that we cannot speak about "holy H_2O," so courage is temperance and this fact is not contradicted by the fact that the soldier's action *is called* "courageous" but not "temperate."

At *Theaetetus* 196e2–6, Plato has Socrates observe the oddity that, while he, Theodorus and Theaetetus do not know what knowledge is (they have not yet been able to define it properly), still, they feel comfortable about saying "This is a case of knowledge, but not that."[19] This seems to show both that they do not know knowledge and that they do know knowledge. The paradox is loosened, I have argued,[20] by distinguishing kinds of knowledge. Socrates and Theaetetus fail to know what knowledge is in the global, comprehensive sense, but they do know what it is locally.

However, to further complicate matters, Socrates himself does seem to allow that "what we say when" is relevant to certain questions about natures. We would say it is unjust to return a man's weapons to him when he is drunk or not in his right mind, and this shows that justice is not simply (as Polemarchus had maintained) "returning what is owed."[21] If there were no contact between philosophical questions and our use of language, we would react to the case Socrates develops by saying, "Oh well. We are not talking about *what we call* 'justice.' We are talking about *what justice is*." On the contrary! —Our theorizing must have *some* contact with our language. Otherwise, the Socratic search after definitions (n. b., definitions *of words*) would be irrelevant to the project of uncovering natures.

Still, we cannot, à la ordinary language philosophy, simply read off what is true and real from "what we say when." We do speak about being overcome by pleasure, but Socrates is skeptical about this (*Protagoras* 352–8). Yet when Polus suggests that they take a survey of the spectators as to whether tyrants have actual power, Socrates scoffs at the suggestion. Polus is just "producing false witnesses against me," Socrates maintains (472bc). And he would, I submit, also say the same of ordinary language objections to his views about *akrasia*, so-called weakness of will.

It is perhaps instructive to consider the case of Evel Knievel. This professional dare devil "challenged himself" to jump on his motorcycle over 12 cars. He then appeared on television, announcing defiantly that he had "never backed down from a challenge" before, and that he was not about to start now. He then jumped over most of the cars (but not all of them), and he broke several bones in the process. Consider the difference between a firefighter who rushes into a burning building to rescue a child, on the one hand, and someone who sets a fire deliberately so that he can rush into the blaze, on the other. People who set fires and then jump into them, people who dare themselves to set up 12 cars and jump over them to meet the "challenge," are not counted as courageous. We think that such people are "mad," as Plato says (350c), that they are reckless and starved for attention. The judgments we make in these cases (this is a case of genuine courage, but not that) are not irrelevant.

The upshot seems to be that the relation between language and reality, between truth and "what we say when," is complex. The behavior of words in the language is *a* consideration, among others, but it is not entirely decisive. By emphasizing the importance of debate and dialectic, Plato may be understood to think that, above all, it is the *reflective* use of words that counts philosophically. But Penner simply *ruling out* issues of what our words mean is surely hasty. Socrates not only appeals to ordinary intuitions—what we would count as a case of X and what we would not—and he does so ubiquitously, but he also seeks definitions—*of words*. We would do well to keep this in mind.

UNITY IN PHILOSOPHY

Charles Kahn develops a unique construal of the doctrine of the unity of the virtues. His well-known view is that other dialogues are shadows cast forward or cast back by *Republic*. He writes, "The key to interpreting Plato's early work is to see that all roads lead to the *Republic*."[22] Reading unity passages in the *Protagoras* in light of passages from *Laws*, Kahn distinguishes sharply between virtue properly so-called and what passes for virtue, what we might call "demotic virtue."[23] To properly apprehend unity, the inquirer needs to have mastered the concepts of unity, plurality, sameness and difference, part and whole, and name and definition[24] (*Laws* 964ab, 965d). Since these abstract matters are uniquely available to philosophers, only philosophers can be properly just, since justice requires knowledge, and the auxiliaries and artisans have only true beliefs, not pieces of knowledge.

But Williams takes issue with this understanding, observing that it is possible to have one element in the soul dominating, while another element rules.[25] The artisan will say to herself, "I am an artisan. *This* is where I fit into the political economy. *This* is why it is crucial that I focus on my own work." This is artisan-wisdom. The soul is properly ordered if reason rules in this way, even though another element dominates. In this way, soldiers and artisans can be just. I concur.

Biconditionality, on which Vlastos pinned his hopes for unity, holds only for philosophers, says Kahn. For ordinary people, operating as they do in the sphere of demotic virtue, it is possible to be brave but intemperate. Thus Kahn. Yet temperance is, we are maintaining, wisdom about what is truly desirable, and a riot in the soul is surely undesirable. Thus, temperance really does require justice, and it does so for everybody, not just for philosophers. When the element of wisdom is subtracted from courage, what remains is demotic courage, bloody-mindedness.

Kahn, like Penner, identifies the relevant kind of knowledge as knowledge of good and evil.[26] Justice "entails the other virtues, enforcing "psychic haermony,"[27] because justice is a functional imperative that each part do its own work, that they work together in harmony. Plato's elaborate scheme of education tames appetite, bringing about psychic harmony. Biconditionality, on which Vlastos pinned his construal of unity, holds, Kan maintains only for philosophers. For ordinary people, trapped in the sphere of demotic virtue, it is possible to be brave but intemperate. Yet temperance, we suppose, is wisdom about what is truly desirable, and a riot in the soul is surely undesirable. So temperance does, after all, imply courage, and it does so for everybody, not just for philosophers. When the element of wisdom is subtracted from courage, what remains is demotic courage, bloody-mindedness.

POWER AS AN EXPLANATION OF UNITY

I will focus primarily in this section on the representation of unity found in Brickhouse and Smith. Others, too, have wanted to cast unity in causal terms, as a "product," a "causal principle," or a "power,"[28] but Brickhouse and Smith offer an especially compelling version of that thesis.

Recognizing the difficulties related to both the equivalence view and the strict identity view, Brickhouse and Smith set out to explain how Socrates could think that virtue is one thing yet also think that the virtues are, to some extent, distinguishable from each other.[29] And drawn by Plato's representation of virtue as a skill,[30] they offer this analogue: as triangulation is applied in both coastal navigation and land surveying, so too, wisdom is applied in both temperance and courage.[31] They represent wisdom as a single state that is *active* in different situations. One might even say that coastal navigation is essentially triangulation *applied* to certain sorts of problems, and in the same way, one might say that courage is essentially wisdom *applied* to certain sorts of situations. This, however, does not mean that the virtues are indistinguishable from one another, for, just as costal navigation and land surveying can surely be distinguished one from the other by the different *work* they do, so too the virtues, as different applications of wisdom, can be distinguished by the different work *they* do.[32] Thus, the virtues are unified in manifesting the same sort of knowledge (wisdom), but they are distinguishable according to the different work that wisdom does in different contexts.[33] Brickhouse and Smith, as well as Cooper, Penner, Frede and Kahn, are drawn by Socrates' example of the definition of "speed" ("the power to do many things in a short time"—*Laches* 192a) to argue that virtue must be *some kind of power*. Each has his own understanding of what that power might be—to produce just "outcomes" (Cooper); to produce virtue-in-persons, immanent virtue (Frede); to produce immanent prudence (Brickhouse and Smith); to produce virtuous acts (Penner); to produce unity (Kahn). But I think the emphasis on power has been overplayed. To conclude on the basis of the fact that the definition of "speed" is the "the power to do many things quickly" that virtue must be some kind of power would be like concluding, because Socrates' example of the kind of definition of "virtue" that he seeks is "shape is the limit of a solid" (*Meno* 76a), that, therefore, virtue must be some kind of *limit* or that it must concern *shape*. Such a move extracts more from the text than is *in* it. Similarly, the fact that Protagoras is pushed into saying that his view that each virtue is distinct comes to the claim that each virtue has its own "power" (330b) does not entail that virtue is some kind of power.

The analogy Brickhouse and Smith appeal to here helps explain how one and the same kind of knowledge can be active in different contexts. But their analogy also faces certain difficulties. To begin with, it does not seem to account for the indispensability of wisdom for virtue. Sailors surely navigated coastlines and governments surely drew boundaries and borderlines long before triangulation had been developed, and this shows that navigation and surveying are possible (though doubtless, clumsier) without triangulation.

That one can navigate without triangulation is shown by the fact that people *did in fact* navigate before triangulation had been developed.

Brickhouse and Smith might reply that they do say that "there is no navigation . . . (of the relevant sort) without triangulation."[34] But the parenthetical qualification fudges the thesis. The "relevant sort" here is specifically *navigation using triangulation*. The claim that *there is no navigation using triangulation without triangulation* is trivial and uninteresting. The truth is that Phoenician sailors navigated coastlines without triangulation, but (what passes for) courageous behavior absent wisdom is, Socrates and Protagoras agree, actually just madness (*Protagoras* 350c).[35]

As I understand Socrates, however, courage just *is* wisdom (about what is genuinely to be feared), and thus, courage, Socrates would say, is strictly *impossible* without wisdom.[36] The relation between triangulation and navigation (etc.) is strictly *disanalogous* to the relation between wisdom and courage with reference to the indispensability of the former phenomenon for the latter. Another problem is that the analogy does not provide us with an account of how a unified whole can have parts.[37] The analogue for triangulation is wisdom, and the analogues for coastal navigation and land surveying are more specific virtues, say, courage and temperance. The problem is that coastal navigation and land surveying are not properly *parts* of triangulation; they are, rather, *applications* of it; however, according to Socrates, courage and temperance are properly *parts* of virtue.[38] The specific virtues are parts of virtue; however, it is hard to see how costal navigation and land surveying can be seen as "pieces" or "parts" of triangulation in this way. Moreover, as I previously argued, courage can be represented as an application of wisdom to dangerous situations and temperance, an application of wisdom to situations of temptation, but justice does not seem to fit the mold, yet justice is undeniably a virtue.[39]

Brickhouse and Smith also maintain that the knowledge that produces pious behavior in pious people is the knowledge of good and evil, but that this is the same knowledge that produces just behavior in just people. But not just knowledge produces virtuous behavior. Nature in people who are naturally temperate produces temperate behavior (and so on, for the other virtues). And again, if Socrates is virtuous, he is not of such a kind by virtue of knowledge of good and evil.[40]

It might be said in defense of Brickhouse and Smith that no analogy is perfect. To say Jones is a mountain of a man does not require that Jones have trees growing out of his shoulders and clouds swirling around his head. It is not required that Jones be like a mountain *in every way*. Similarly, to say that virtue is like triangulation does not require that virtue be like triangulation *in every respect*. But we must judge the success of the effort of Brickhouse and

Smith in this regard by examining the analogy they offer. And the analogy they offer turns out to be serviceable in one respect but not in another.

It is a natural tendency for us to substitute analogies for Plato's analogies which we scholars find more congenial for explaining the unity of the virtues—more congenial, that is, than parts of a face or "parts" of a lump of gold. The unity of the virtues is not quite like the facial unity of the parts of a face, and not quite like the unity of a lump of gold—it is more like a skill unity, like triangulation. I myself was at one time drawn to represent the unity of the virtues in relation to the world. Things in the Northern Hemisphere behave differently than do things in the Southern Hemisphere,[41] so that there are real differences between the hemispheres. Yet we recognize that the hemispheres of the world are finally parts of the world, inseparable from it. Just so, I once thought, justice and temperance are inseparable from virtue. This analogy, too, is at first attractive—but no one would dream of claiming that the Northern hemisphere *is* the Southern Hemisphere, or that the Northern Hemisphere *is* the world.

Having abandoned the hemispheres of the world as analogous to the virtues, I more recently thought that the virtues might be one from one point of view and many from another, not unlike a marriage. Suppose that Jones and Smith are married. We can and do assess their marriage as an element not reducible to Jones or to Smith. Jones and Smith, as individuals, may be happy, but we also characterize their union as happy; we speak about "happy marriages." (And unhappy ones, too.) Another parallel is that we might say that we cannot fully appreciate Jones apart from his marriage to Smith. They are both two and one. Still, no one would argue that Jones *is* Smith or that Smith *is* Jones, or that *Jones* "what he is" reduces without remainder to *the husband of Smith*. Yet we are supposed to be tempted to say that courage *is* virtue.

UNITY AND THE DUCK-RABBIT

Another possible analogue is the duck-rabbit. Just as, it might be said, one figure presents two distinct interpretations, so one thing, a good character, manifests itself in two ways, now as courage, now again as temperance. And staring at the duck-rabbit, one can experience that one figure flashing back and forth from one interpretation to the other.

This is as close as I, at any rate, can come to what Plato would require. Yet, although it is true that one set of lines can be understood in two different ways here, still, no one is tempted to think that the duck *is* the rabbit—yet we are supposed to think that courage is wisdom, and that piety is justice—or to think that the duck is the duck-rabbit—yet we are supposed to think that courage *is* the whole of virtue. The analogy, again, works in some ways and in some ways, it does not work.

Figure 4.1. The Muller Optical Illusion.
Source: Public Domain

We are tempted as scholars to patch up Plato, to suggest analogies that did not occur to him, but the analogies others have tried, as well as the analogies I myself have tried, seem to fail at crucial points. It might be, of course, that there is a perfect analogy that has simply not occurred to any of us yet. But the other possibility is that Plato (as I understand him) is right: The virtues are one and they are many, and the way in which this unity-and-diversity is manifested truly is *sui generis*.

Chapter Five

Other Indications of Ineffability

As already noted, a danger of specifying what cannot be said is that the statement that such-and-such cannot be said appears to be caught in its own echo. For this reason, I think, Plato *hints* at his position that the unity thesis is ineffable without trying directly to argue for it, indeed, without stating it at all. And another reason for avoiding addressing the topic directly is that it would be out of character for Socrates, who denies having wisdom about things "great or small" (*Apology* 21d) to float an entire theory of language and an entire theory of mind. Socrates may, and, I think, *does* have in mind—so to speak, *at the back* of his mind—big theoretical theses, among them, arguably, a coherence theory of truth,[1] yet if one were to ask him "What is the nature of truth?" he would surely reply "I do not know." Socrates for logical reasons and early Plato for literary reasons both avoid raising large metaphysical issues directly.

One way Plato suggests ineffability in relation to the unity of the virtues is by deliberately fumbling with his phraseology.[2] The ham-fistedness that characterizes both Protagoras' and Socrates' speech is not, I think, indicative of any particular weakness on the part of either character in the dialogue,[3] nor is it a consequence of Plato's immaturity as a writer at the time he wrote the dialogue. Rather, it is an indication of the obscurity of the topic at hand. After all, everyone allows that Protagoras' long speech at 320c–328d is a fine composition. It is hardly the work of an immature writer. And again, as Socrates enters the scene in Callias' house, Prodicus is holding forth on some topic or other, but Socrates tells us, Prodicus has such a deep, booming voice that it "set[s] off a kind of rumbling echo in the room, and I could not understand a word" (316a). The important part of this passage, as I see things, is not so much the cause as it is the effect: no one can understand a word of what Prodicus is saying. Later, it emerges, according to Protagoras, that Homer,

Hesiod and Simonides were in fact sophists who disguised themselves as poets because they were embarrassed to reveal their true calling (316d). Unlike them, Protagoras is not shy about identifying himself as a sophist (317bc). Hippocrates, however, is embarrassed to admit that he wants to study with Protagoras in order to become a sophist himself (311).[4] Socrates indicates that he thinks Protagoras' real motive for inviting Hippias, Callias, Alcibiades and Prodicus to join them is to parade his own prowess before them (317c). So we have one sophist whom no one can understand, other sophists hiding their real profession, a potential student hiding his motive for studying, and we have Protagoras hiding his real motives. Deception is rampant. What lies behind the veil? It is appropriate that a dialogue that features a thesis that is beyond the scope of language should contain such instances of the appearance/ reality dialectic, for that thesis is itself *veiled.*

As for the topic over which Protagoras and Socrates contend, it, too, is identified by a series of *gestures*. Protagoras, in his long speech explaining why virtue is (thought by Athenians to be) teachable, says there is "one thing, one essential thing," then, in his explanation of his position, he lists *several* things—" justice and moderation and piety and virtue" (324e–325a). Protagoras, who prides himself on precision, cannot seem to locate the object he wants to discuss, as though he, too, is "hunting for the right words and has not yet found them."[5] Socrates suggests to Protagoras that he, like Socrates himself, "should say . . . that justice is holy and holiness just . . . if you would allow me, I should say the same for you, that justice is *either the same thing as* piety or *very much like it*" (331ab). The two are arguing over a question neither of them seems quite able to formulate properly. Protagoras, a moment later, maintains vaguely that there is *some* difference between holiness and justice, but then he adds, "However, what does it matter? If you like, then assume justice is holy and holiness just" (331c). Socrates, of course, has no interest in a discussion on the basis of "if you like. . . ." However, phrases like "*some* difference," "What does it matter?" "If you like, then assume . . ." *gesture in the direction of* their target, but without *pointing to* it. When Socrates tries to show Protagoras that there are important lines of connection between temperance and wisdom, Protagoras replies that everything is similar to everything else in some way or other; "white resembles black," he says, "and hard, soft" (331d). Socrates asks, then, if there is only a *slight* resemblance between temperance and wisdom, and Protagoras replies, "Not quite that, but not in the way you believe, either" (331e).[6] Such vagueness would be intolerable if it were not necessary. And again, at 333b, Socrates demands, "Must not temperance and wisdom be the same, just as justice and piety turned out to be *much the same* earlier?" The fact that the analogies Protagoras and Socrates adopt are not terribly apt and the fact that they cannot seem to identify the bone of contention between them indicate that the topic is obscure.

Another element Plato keeps hidden in the early dialogues is his theory of truth. I have argued[7] that, at the tail end of his career, Socrates, who has been largely absent for a long while,[8] returns to action in the *Philebus*, armed with his method. He says of the Socratic elenchos,[9] "There is no way a better method than this, the one that I have always loved, though often in the past, it has left me isolated and confused" (16b). Plato returns to Socrates and to his method with love and enthusiasm, I submit, because he has, over the years, worked out the machinery necessary to support that method. He has carved out a theory of forms, so that Socrates and his interlocutors will have something stable to talk *about*. Honest philosopher that he is, Plato faces difficulties for *this version* of the theory of forms, but he has Socrates portrayed as a teenager in the critical dialogue, *Parmenides*. He can be taken, then, to be saying, "You must have a theory of forms.[10] But don't have an adolescent theory. Have a mature theory."[11] He works out the image metaphysics of the *Timaeus* as a more supple theory than the participation metaphysics of *Republic*. He posits the uniqueness of the system of forms through the device of the Form of the Good, in order to circumvent relativist objections ("You have your coherent system, and I have mine"), since the system of interrelated types is the best (and hence, the uniquely possible) system.[12] The coherence theory of truth, then, underwrites Socratic method. There is one and only one fully consistent set of beliefs, and those are the true ones. If my beliefs are demonstrably consistent, while yours are demonstrably inconsistent, this indicates that you are wrong and at least gives me confidence that I am right, and this is the lynchpin of Socratic method. Having worked out what is required to support that method, Plato represents Socrates returning to that method in his penultimate dialogue, *Philebus*, confident that he will not now be left by it "confused and isolated."

Another uncertain element in the dialogues concerns recollection. In the *Meno*, it is maintained that coming to understand what virtue really is is like being reminded of something we knew previously but have now forgotten. Socrates says that, according to certain priests and priestesses, we do not really die. Our souls are simply re-incarnated upon what we call "death." We have existed before this lifetime. Being re-born has caused us to forget what we knew in our former lifetimes. Yet what we knew before has left behind traces in our minds, and by following these trails, we can "recollect" what we have "forgotten."

Plato leaves it at this, but we can supplement the text a bit. Like striving to remember something we have forgotten, in struggling to understand virtue, we have the sense that we know—we just cannot seem to put our finger on what we seek to recover. When we hear a wrong answer,[13] we know right away that this is wrong, even though we do not yet know what the right answer is. This is possible only because deeply, we do already know what the right answer is. Finally, when we arrive at the right answer, it has a feeling of familiarity. We say to ourselves, "Of course! I knew it all along!"[14]

But Socrates does not want to get drawn into a discussion about the afterlife, especially with Meno, a man who delights in memorizing other people's stories.[15] So Socrates expresses uncertainty about the priestly story concerning re-incarnation, saying instead that he is confident that we will be better if we believe it than if we do not (86bc). The reincarnation story is one Plato himself doubtless subscribes to, but in the *Meno*, it has the status of a metaphor. It is *as if* we are striving to recollect something we knew but have now forgotten. Plato's position on the unity and the diversity of the virtues is like Socrates' answer to Meno's Paradox. It is not strictly true that we either know or we do not know. The truth is that in a way, we know and, in a way, we do not know. Just so, in a way, the virtues are one and, in a way, they are many. How exactly this works is a topic Plato leaves at the level of metaphor in the *Meno*. (It is *as if* we are striving to remember something we have forgotten.) And in the *Protagoras*, though he arguably thinks that the virtues are one in a way and that they are many in a way, he abandons the question in that dialogue, and at the tail end of his career, he is still scratching his head over the question.

Returning to the *Protagoras*, then, in a way, the virtues are one, and in a way, they are many. Beyond the trouble that Protagoras and Socrates experience over words, various dramatic elements also reveal deception, indirection, or lack of clarity. Socrates asks Protagoras to confine himself to brief answers, forgoing long speeches, but Protagoras bristles at the suggestion that Socrates should set the ground-rules for the discussion. Alcibiades intervenes (as do various others), striving to make arrangements under which the discussion can continue. Alcibiades indicates that, in his judgment at least, Protagoras' prolixity is a trick. He "meets every question with a long oration, eluding the arguments and refusing to meet them properly, spinning [things] out until most of his hearers have forgotten what the question was" (336cd). What appears to be eloquence is in fact a ruse. The Spartans, says Socrates, who (allegedly) were philosophically inclined, led the rest of the Greeks to think they were nothing but overly enthusiastic warriors. Then, when everyone had been lulled into expecting nothing terribly illuminating from them, the Spartans would send forth a shaft of perception, a "telling phrase" (342e), dazzling everyone. As the Sophists strive to create the appearance of wisdom, so the Spartans strive to create the appearance of brutishness. It is not clear how seriously Plato intends the claim of Spartan acumen,[16] but it accounts for

Simonides presenting a philosophical argument disguised as a poem (344b). Things are not what they seem. Socrates regards what seems right to him, *viz.*, the Socratic paradox that no one does wrong willingly, as a view with which all wise men agree (345e). Yet in the *Gorgias*, Polus snorts at the idea; he claims that everyone disagrees with Socrates (473de). Surely, Polus is right about this. To preserve the fact, then, that most people disagree with Socrates and the claim that the wise think the contrary, we shall have to maintain that all wise people *deeply* agree with Socrates. Since it is possible for one to entertain false beliefs about what one believes, Socrates could maintain that wise people *who believe* that they disagree with him actually, *deeply*, agree with him. (The alternative would be that those who disagree with him are only apparently wise, but this would be remarkably uncharitable.) When it comes to the Socratic paradox, the *many* say that we are often overcome by pleasure. But, Socrates maintains, this is an extremely *loose* way of speaking (358d); in fact, it is strictly *false*.[17] No one, faced with a choice between two evils, will knowingly select the greater of the two. Cowardice and rashness both exhibit ignorance, while courage exhibits understanding. Apparent courage without understanding is really just "madness" (350c).[18] Once we see things clearly, once we "work out the reason" (*Meno* 98e3–4), we agree. Altogether, then, several dramatic elements suggest an implicit distinction between appearance and reality, shadow and substance. This shifting, this uncertainty, is particularly appropriate, I think, in a dialogue whose topic is one that cannot properly be *named*.

Suppose that a strange creature is discovered in the wilds of Australia. It looks like a wild dog. It behaves, pretty much, like a dog behaves but with this difference: it purrs. Is it a cat that looks like a dog, or is it a dog that behaves like a cat? We are not sure. Now then, what is the referent of "it" in *It looks like a dog*? What is the referent of "it" in *It purrs*? *It* does not refer to the dog or to the cat—the reference is to *that non-descript beast*, the one about which a classificatory question has been raised. If eventually, a consensus emerges among zoologists and we collectively decide that the animal is a dog, then "It looks like a dog" as well as "It purrs" will be *about the dog*. But until the classificatory question has been resolved, the referent of "it" in "It purrs" will be *that strange animal*. One feels like gesturing—" *That there animal. That*'s what we are talking about."

Similarly, all Plato can do is to *gesture* towards the question he wants to address. The one is the many and the many are one. How is this possible? It can't even be stated, let alone thought. Plato tries out a couple of metaphors, neither of which is terribly successful, and he drops the question in the end. (And he is still troubled by the issue at the end of his career.) Plato scholars have tried their hands at delivering their own illustrations—the virtues are like species under a genus, or like the hemispheres of the world, or like applications of a skill, or like married people—but none of these seems entirely adequate either. So maybe Plato is right—the way in which the virtues are one and many must be *experienced*. It cannot be argued for; it cannot even be stated. As Wittgenstein writes, "So in the end, when one is doing philosophy, one gets to the point where one would like just to emit an inarticulate sound."[19]

Chapter Six

Meaning and Express-ability

At *Cratylus* 427e, Plato indicates that words should have hidden in them the essences of the things they name. I assume that being unified is a non-accidental, i.e., a necessary, feature of the virtues. If the virtues really are unified, then, it seems, that unity ought to be present in the word, *aretē*. But I am maintaining that the unity of the virtues is ineffable, i.e., real but stubbornly resistant to coherent articulation.[1] This is why Plato, in writing *Protagoras*, fumbles for words; it is why he *gestures* towards his thesis with images. The question thus presents itself whether or not the idea that there is an essential feature of virtue that cannot be spoken is inconsistent with the idea that the word, *aretē*, like all words, should somehow contain within itself the essence of its referent. How can it embody that essence if part of the essence is beyond expression?

I answer this objection by observing that the *Cratylus* doctrine requires only that a word should contain *some measure* of what it refers to or picks out. It is not required that each word pick out *the whole of* its referent, just that there be some direct relation between word and object. If whole natures and nothing but natures of kinds were revealed in the names for those kinds, then *there would be no need for us to study kinds*. We could ignore the forms. We could simply read off the natures of things from our words. That we are enjoined nevertheless to study forms (*Cratylus* 439c–440d), that names convey essences *only in outline* (432e–433e), and that the name-giver's work can and should be scrutinized to determine how *accurate* it was (436b)—all these features of the passage show that the name may not reveal the whole nature of the referent. One shortcoming of the name-giver, for example, is that he seems to have been overly impressed with flux and not enough impressed by stability (436a ff.). Part of the nature of a kind of thing is revealed in its name, but there is no requirement that any name be both *complete* and correct with regard to the full nature of its designatum. While it is true that the word *aretē* should reveal part of the nature of its designatum, it is not inconsistent with the *Cratylus'* doctrine to claim, as I do, that the name *arête* does not, because it could not, reveal the unity of its object.

It is true that at *Charmides* 159a, Plato maintains that what we think, we must be able to say. And again, at *Laches* 190c, we are told, "What we know, we must . . . be able to state." So if we either know or merely think that the virtues are one and many, it might be said, then we should be able to say this as well. But the unity of the virtues is not something we can directly express or even arguably think; it is something we finally must *see*. At *Laws* 965b,[2] Plato writes that the guardians, the *phulakai, analogous to the eye* in the human body, must *look* (*blepein*) from the "dissimilar many to the one form" (965c). The guardians will "adequately grasp (*hikanōs hexein*) the nature of virtue . . . whether it is many or . . . one" (965e). The Athenian Stranger asks, "Can anyone get a more accurate view [*akribestera skepsis*] than by being able to look (*blepein*) from the many dissimilar to the one unifying form?" (965c). The guardians "must be constrained . . . *to see* exactly [*akribōs idein*] what is the identity permeating all the four [virtues], the unity to be found . . . alike in courage, in temperance, in justice, in wisdom, and entitling them all to be called by the one name, 'virtue'" (965cd). Unity is something we finally must *look for* and *see*. It is also significant that in *Republic*, Plato defines the individual, so-called "cardinal," virtues—courage (429c), temperance (431e–432a), wisdom (428b ff.) and justice (434–5)—*but nowhere in the corpus does he properly define "virtue."*

The *Meno*, it is true, initially aims to define "virtue." The dialogue begins with the claim that we cannot know how virtue is acquired unless and until we know what it is (71b), and the first part of that dialogue witnesses several failed attempts by Meno to define "virtue." But having failed himself to define the word, Meno hijacks the discussion, demanding that they return to his question, *How is virtue acquired?* (86cd), and Socrates, with considerable grumbling, complies with this demand, relying on the "hypothesis" that virtue is knowledge (86e). That view is dispatched when it is recalled that virtuous fathers, who teach their sons everything else, often fail to teach them virtue, and it seems to follow that virtue cannot be taught (93a ff.). (Virtuous fathers would teach virtue if they could, so, since they do not teach it, it seems to follow that it cannot be taught.) Since virtue crucially involves wisdom, and since no one is wise at birth (99ab), it follows that virtue must be acquired—that it is not innate. It seems to follow that virtue is learned but not taught.[3] Nevertheless, we never *do* get a proper definition of "virtue" in this dialogue, and the issue does not come up again in the corpus. If it is of the nature of the virtues that they are unified, then an adequate definition will parade that unity. That Plato makes only this one foray at defining "virtue," that that attempt fails, that he never revisits the task, and that the real nature of virtue is so central a part of his philosophy suggest that "virtue" cannot, in his considered judgment, be properly defined at all. Because the real nature of virtue is elusive, we resort to "poems and songs, pipings and dancing and harping" (348a). One such literary work, one such "song," I think, is the *Protagoras* itself. Poetry must be treated cautiously, and the detailed analysis of the "Song" of Simonides shows that we cannot take things at face value. But with sufficient concentration and effort on our part, poetry may reveal to us things that argument cannot. It can enhance our *vision*.

A definition must have the proper scope (*Meno* 73d and 78c); it must name the essential feature, and not just a characteristic accompaniment of the definiens (*Euthyphro* 9d); it must square more or less with our pre-reflective intuitions (*Charmides* 159c ff.); and it must be non-circular (*Meno* 73a, 78d).[4] If what we can think, we can say, and if we cannot say what virtue is (we can only *see* it), it follows that we cannot *think* what virtue is, either. And in *Republic*, when the philosopher experiences the whole array of the forms, that *experience* is specifically represented or cast as a *vision* (*Republic* 540). It is not something the philosopher rationally discovers or apprehends; it is something she *sees*. Consider that a proper definition of "virtue" would have to include all of its essential features, including its unity and its diversity. Yet because this aspect of virtue cannot be spoken, it cannot be thought. It can only be *seen*. (Again, see *Laws* 965a.) This, then, is why we never do get a definition of "virtue." Any such definition would have to include an articulation of its unity/diversity, and this feature cannot properly be expressed. For this reason, the definition would be radically incomplete. It would fail the *scope* test.

Having apparently answered Meno's Paradox with the story told by the priestly caste, to the effect that, rather than dying, our souls simply get recycled, so that we can, with sufficient effort, "recollect" what we knew in our former lives but have now "forgotten," Socrates proceeds with the slave boy demonstration to show that we can, without having been taught, come to recognize things we knew (deeply) but are unaware of knowing. Yet when that point has been secured, Socrates backs away from the priestly story. Not only will he not argue for it; he will not even "confidently assert" it to be true (86b6). Given the ubiquity of the reincarnation story in the dialogues—again, it is present in *Meno*, *Phaedo*, *Republic* X, *Gorgias*, *Phaedrus* and *Laws* X— it seems to me extremely likely that Plato himself believed that we are reincarnated. Although he does not experience trouble stating the story, he does apparently think it cannot be argued for.[5] It is beyond the reach of the *logos*.

In *Republic,* Plato refuses to define the Form of the Good, representing Socrates as asking, "Have you not noticed that beliefs in the absence of knowledge are all shameful and ugly things, since the best of them are blind?" (506c). Rather than attempting to define the Form of the Good, Socrates compares the good to the sun, its "offspring" and "the thing most like it." The Form of the Good, as Santas has argued,[6] consists in the form-being of all of the forms. All just things participate in the form of justice, and the form of justice and the form of temperance, in their form-being, both participate in the Form of the Good. The Form of the Good, as Santas elegantly puts it, is the proper attribute of the formal attributes of all the other forms.[7] If *what the Form of the Good is* cannot even in principle be articulated, Socrates is right that neither he nor anyone else properly knows what it is. But it is the ground of everything else, so it is real. It is real but ineffable.[8] Any definition we offer is going to be partial and incomplete.

And again, in *Theaetetus,* having determined that knowledge is not just whatever one thinks (it must also be true), and that it is not just something true that one thinks (it must also involve a *logos* or account), Socrates sets out to discover what giving an account might consist in. But he indicates considerable hesitation about the project, since it requires that he give an account of *giving an account.* If he is not yet sure what giving an account comes to, how can he give an account of giving an account (206d ff.)?[9] Like many fascinating questions in *Theaetetus,* this one is dropped, but it does raise a series of perplexing questions: Can one give an explanation of giving an explanation? Can one develop a theory of developing theories? If these questions are to be answered negatively, then, while it is clear that there is something properly called "giving an account," no account of it can be given. It is real, but ineffable.

And again, in *Phaedrus* 274b–279c, Socrates demurs setting out his views about the just and the good and the beautiful, the "deepest parts of" his doctrine. He claims that he writes what he writes rather to "treasure up reminders for [him]self . . . and for others who follow the same path" (276d). The business of written philosophy is actually the business of "planting and sowing in a fitting soul intelligent words that are able to help" readers recover what lies hidden in their own souls already. It has been argued[10] that among the deepest parts of the doctrine is Plato's theory of truth. He does not undertake to specify what he takes to be the nature of truth because such an undertaking would require him to try to say something true about all true things, and, like giving an account of an giving an account or providing an explanation for providing an explanation, so, too, saying a true thing about all true things is something that cannot be done. This is not to say that there is no such thing as truth.[11] Of course, there is. It simply cannot be articulated. If Plato concludes that certain matters cannot be coherently articulated, then the category of things that are a) real and b) important but c) not expressible is *non-empty*. It is not entirely surprising that the unity of the virtues might emerge as such an issue. This, of course, does not establish that the unity of the virtues is ineffable, but it does show that elsewhere in the corpus, Plato makes theoretical room for things beyond the reach of discourse.

Chapter Seven

Socratic Intellectualism

Socrates thinks that no one does the wrong thing willingly or knowingly. This doctrine has come to be known among scholars the "the Socratic Paradox."[1] If anyone did the wrong thing with her eyes fully open, she would be harming herself intentionally, and nobody wants to do this. People do the wrong thing, quite frequently in fact, but it is because they do not fully understand what they are doing. Evils could be avoided, write Brickhouse and Smith, if only we would heed the Delphic injunction.[2] When we apply this claim to the virtues, the result is that no one is deliberately, knowingly vicious. If the coward really understood what cowardice really is, she would never be drawn to it. People are vicious because they are ignorant.[3]

Now, it is possible, evidently, to be virtuous without knowing what virtue is. Socrates, Plato clearly wants us to think, is virtuous, but he says he "know[s] nothing whatsoever about virtue" (*Meno* 71a). He says at *Charmides* 165bc that he does not know what *sōphrosynē* is, but he displays this very virtue when Alcibiades tries to seduce him in *Symposium* (219bd); indeed, he manifests that virtue in the *Charmides* itself, when he maintains his composure as Charmides' robe (accidentally?) flies open (155d5–6). He tells Lysis and Menexenus that the others will laugh at them, because, while they consider themselves friends, they do not know what friendship is (*Lysis* 223b). But he does not deny that they *are* friends—indeed, he says, "I put myself among you [as a friend]" (223b). He says he cannot know whether the just person is better off than the unjust person until he knows what justice is (*Republic* 354c), but he does not deny that the just person is better off. The just person is better off than the unjust person, and, as previously mentioned, Socrates, Menexenus and Lysis are friends, but Socrates does not know these things unless and until he knows what justice and friendship *are*.

Even if we do not *know* (in the strict Socratic sense of that word) what the virtues are, if we do possess them, we apparently should have some sense of their natures. Our minds should not be complete blank when we hear the words "courage," "justice," and so forth.[4] Having been assured by Critias that young Charmides is outstandingly temperate, Socrates tells the young man that, since he is temperate, he must have "some opinion of temperance" (*Charmides* 158e–159a). This claim should be taken with several grains of salt, however. Critias himself was later one of the Thirty, and because of his sanguinary character, became known as "*the* tyrant."[5] Charmides was later to become one of "Ten of the Piraeus."[6] They are two men in Greek political history who are notorious for exhibiting no patience or self-control. So, Socrates' apparent claim that Charmides must know what temperance is needs to be understood against the background knowledge that Charmides himself was notoriously *in*temperate. Still, Meno, who seems in his discussion with Socrates to be cagey and dishonest, is the young man Socrates asks about the nature *of virtue*. Yet, via the recollection hypothesis, even Meno knows (deeply) what virtue is. So Critias and Charmides must also know (deeply) what *sōphrosynē* is—otherwise, there would be no point in asking them about it.[7] Since we all know (deep down) what the virtues are, when we entertain false beliefs about the virtues (like the belief that justice is the advantage of the stronger), we are in fact *lying* to ourselves.

Again, Socrates says he does not know what courage is (*Laches* 290e), but he shows great courage in facing his own execution, refusing to try to escape prison. Laches himself testifies about the courage Socrates showed at Delium (*Laches* 181b). And at *Charmides* 157–8, Socrates suggests that an agent might be temperate by nature, having inherited the trait. Critias has told him that Charmides is legendary for his temperance, and Socrates attributes this characteristic to his lineage. The point is not pursued, but, I imagine, just as some children are by nature robust and pugnacious, so some children might not be tempted by the pleasures of the flesh. If one is temperate by nature, one is temperate, but one does not need to know, in the sense that Socrates is pushing, what temperance *is*.

Moreover, even if one cannot define "courage" adequately, one still might count as knowing what virtue is, provided that one can point to someone whom one has made virtuous (*Laches* 185e).[8] And returning to two texts previously mentioned, Socrates tells Lysis that the others will laugh at Lysis, Menexenus and Socrates himself, since they think they are friends, but they do not know what friendship is, but he does not deny that they *are* friends (*Lysis* 223b); and Socrates says he cannot know whether the just person is better off that the unjust person until he knows what justice is (*Republic* 354c), but he does not deny that the just person *is* better off. That one can be virtuous by nature and that one can know what virtue is without being able to define "virtue"—one can have what we might call "virtual knowledge" of it—make the view that Socratic ethics is strictly intellectualist—the view that one must be smart to be good— somewhat dubious.

Although virtue does not entail knowledge, knowledge does seem to entail virtue. When Glaucon revives Thrasymachus' cynical theory of justice, he presents the case with considerable energy and aplomb. Glaucon compares the just person to the unjust person vià the Gyges' ring case, and Socrates remarks, "How vigorously you polish the people in this competition!" (361d). Glaucon seems to be *drawn* to the cynical view, though he valiantly resists it (358cd). Yet once he sees justice and injustice for what they really are, he is no longer even tempted by Thrasymachus' view (and neither, indeed, is Thrasymcahus himself [498cd, 612b]). When we come to see things clearly, we no longer want the things we wanted when we were ignorant. Desire is educable.[9]

Socrates' view, that virtue is wisdom, only implies that virtue can be taught if it is assumed that:

[*Assumption 1*] All wisdom is something that can be taught.

Yet, while it is clear that all knowledge is something that can be taught, this does not seem to be true of wisdom. Protagoras, meanwhile, maintains that virtue is not wisdom, but this only implies that virtue cannot be taught if it is assumed that

[*Assumption 2*] No non-wisdom can be taught.

But surely, one can be taught a skill, for example, proficiency in Morse code, without thereby becoming wise. Wisdom and knowledge are both acquired—babies are not wise or knowledgeable[10]—but wisdom seems to be *inward* in a way that makes it unsusceptible to *reliable* teaching.

Now then, the Reversal in the *Protagoras* occurs when Socrates imagines a reified *logos* upbraiding both Protagoras and Socrates himself. The *logos* says, "One of you, having said at the outset that virtue is not teachable, now is contradicting himself by maintaining that . . . [the virtues are knowledge]—which is the best way to show that virtue is teachable.[11] If virtue is something other than knowledge, as Protagoras tried to establish, then, obviously, it could not be taught"[12] (361ab). But the *Logos*' argument *requires* that all and only knowledge (or wisdom) can be taught, and this is far from clear. If this undefended assumption is scuttled, if knowledge is clearly demarcated from wisdom, then we can grant that all knowledge is teachable without saying the same for wisdom. After all, part of Socrates' wisdom comes from obeying the promptings of the daimonion, but these are not anything Socrates has *earned*.

The voice just *speaks* occasionally to Socrates. Because the daimonion phenomenon is rare (*Apology* 40a3–4), Socrates cannot teach another person to heed his own daimonion, for the other person probably does not *have* one.[13] This element in Socratic wisdom cannot be taught. And the moral Socrates claims to draw from Simonides' poem is that it is possible to be in the process of *becoming* good, but that it is not possible altogether *to be* good (344de). Being good would require being thoroughly wise, and "only the god is really wise" (*Apology* 23a). *Being* good is another wisdom-element that cannot be taught. It appears from these two cases that not all wisdom can be taught.

A rather different explanation of the Reversal appears in Frede. To recap, *I* think that Socrates objects to Protagoras' claim that virtue can be taught, not because he doubts that virtue is wisdom, but precisely because he conceives of virtue as wisdom which, he thinks, is unlike knowledge in that it cannot be reliably taught. Frede thinks Socrates acts as Hippocrates' guardian throughout the dialogue, testing Protagoras to determine whether he has the expertise he represents himself as having. Protagoras switches his position, Frede maintains, because the view that special expertise is required of good citizens (these are what he claims regularly to be able to produce [319a]) is undemocratic.[14] Since Protagoras feels compelled to misrepresent his actual view, the anti-Protagorean argument Socrates develops is ad hominem.[15] He refutes Protagoras the man, but not Protagoreanism. Socrates challenges the view that virtue is teachable in order to expose Protagoras' shallowness. So the Reversal is apparent only—Socrates only *pretends* to think that virtue is not knowledge, though he really does not doubt this, and Protagoras feels that *he* must pretend that he believes that no special expertise is required for good citizenship so as to avoid appearing anti-democratic. Thus, Frede.

Plato's attitude towards democracy, however, is not at all simple. Middle Plato thinks democracy appeals to the lowest part of the soul, since the Many vote on the basis of *what they want* (*Republic* VIII, 557). On the other hand, the Laws of Athens ask if Socrates is content living under their authority, observing that, if he violently disapproved, he was always free to leave. Socrates answers that he was more or less contended (*Crito* 51de). While it is clear that middle Plato is no advocate of democracy, it is also plain that he opposes the seizure of power by violence, à la the Thirty. The tyrant is the worst sort of human being, and tyranny is the worst sort of regime. Additionally, Plato writes that there will be no end to troubles until rulers become philosophers, or philosophers become rulers (*Republic* 473cd). Since the many regard philosophers as impractical cranks (see 488a, the analogy to the riotous crew on the ship), the possibility of the many selecting a philosopher as a ruler is, in fact, negligible.[16] So Plato must be pinning his hopes on rulers becoming philosophers.[17] This is what appeared to be happening for a time at Syracuse, but Dion, tyrant of Syracuse, in the end refused any further instruction.[18]

Altogether, the kallipolis can't be just a dream or "prayer" (*euchē*) (450d, 456b), but its realization, its full instantiation, is extremely unlikely. Yet if it were to come about, it appears that the kallipolis might come into being democratically. An elected official might become a philosopher. Indeed, I think, the political arrangements of the kallipolis (those who are wise in charge, those who are courageous coming to the aid of those who are wise in properly controlling those dominated by desire, etc.) may be regarded as software that may be plugged into several different kinds of hardware (kingship, representative democracy, etc.). In any case, because the kallipolis is so remote a possibility, we should focus our energy on building the ideal city within our own souls (591e, 592ab).[19]

Because Plato's attitude towards democracy is complex, there is no simple reading of his representation of Protagoras' relation to it. It is not given in the text that Protagoras fears expressing undemocratic ideas. But I grant that this fear is pretty clearly present elsewhere in the corpus. According to some scholars, when Socrates asks Gorgias if he will teach justice to his students so that they will not misuse the oratorical skill he teaches them (460a4–5), Gorgias must resist replying, "I don't give a hoot about justice. I am only here in Athens to make money."[20] This kind of hesitation to say what one really believes is arguably present in the *Gorgias*, but I find no evidence for it in the *Protagoras*[21] Kahn[22] maintains that Socrates' argument in the *Gorgias*, since it relies on a premise which Gorgias is compelled to concede for political reasons, is ad hominem.[23]

Frede's hypothesis, that the Reversal comes about because Protagoras feels compelled to cover up his real, undemocratic ideas, is unsupported, and the Reversal is better illuminated by positing Plato's gathering uncertainty about Assumptions 1 and 2. These assumptions certainly are challenged later in the corpus, especially in *Republic*. In the *Protagoras*, I think, Plato is probing his own growing discomfort with strictly Socratic philosophy.

Beyond this, Socrates early on expresses his uncertainty about whether virtue can be taught. At 319a, Socrates compliments Protagoras on having mastered the political art, on being an expert on "making men good citizens"—then he adds, "*if* indeed you have mastered it." He continues, "I did not think it was something that could be taught." At 329b, he says roundly, "I do not believe that virtue can be taught." If we take these expressions of uncertainty to apply not only to temperance and courage but also to wisdom, not only to the moral virtues, but also to the intellectual virtue,[24] then the game is over. In this event, Socrates does not believe that wisdom can be taught. And even if we do not take these statements to apply to all virtues, insofar as courage is represented as wisdom about the things that are dreadful, it would follow that, since (moral) virtue cannot be taught, at least *this kind of wisdom* also cannot be taught. Even if philosophical wisdom could be taught, Socrates' view appears to be that strictly *moral* wisdom cannot be.

Now, I do grant that Socratic ethics tends to be intellectualist, as if the only motives for the actions we perform were beliefs.[25] People act badly, Socrates thinks, only out of ignorance. On this showing, since virtue is wisdom, and since, while knowledge can be reliably taught, wisdom cannot be, it would follow that virtue cannot be taught.

Frede's explanation of the Reversal, though possible, is unsupported by the text. We are not treated to Protagoras fretting about offending democrats anywhere in the dialogue. Beyond this, the Reversal might be accounted for in the following way. It might be that Plato is beginning to feel uncomfortable about assumptions 1 and 2, and that he seeks dialectically to call these into question. Maybe being wise involves more than knowing things; maybe it does not even require knowing things. Socrates strongly denies knowing anything at all about virtue (*Meno* 71a), but he does admit to possessing "perhaps a human wisdom" (*Apology* 20d). So wisdom and knowledge are not, evidently, co-extensive. In *Republic*, the auxiliaries, whose leading, kind-making virtue is courage, still have only true beliefs about what is truly dreadful. They must be told what is truly dreadful by the rulers, those who are properly wise in these things. The behavior of the auxiliaries *manifests* wisdom, but the auxiliaries themselves would, as Vlastos says, flunk an elenctic examination on the nature of courage.[26]

The relation between knowledge, ignorance and virtue, then, is complex. It is possible to be virtuous without knowing (in the strict Socratic sense of that word) what virtue is. But if an agent *does* know what virtue is, then the agent will be virtuous. No one wants to harm herself. When people do the wrong thing, when people exhibit viciousness, it is because they are ignorant. To Molly Bloom's question, "What am I to do with all these desires?' Plato's Socrates would answer, "Think! Think about what you really want, think about what kind of person you really want to be." To this extent, Socratic ethics seems to be intellectualist. Yet Socrates warns Crito never to do wrong voluntarily (*Crito* 49a) and he congratulates himself on never having done so (*Apology* 37a, *Gorgias* 488a). Neither the warning not to do wrong voluntarily nor the self-congratulation on never having done so would make sense unless it were possible to do wrong voluntarily.[27]

The political arm of Plato's project in *Republic* is to run the polis in as deliberate, intelligent and careful a manner as is possible. As part of this aim, future rulers are subjected to ten years of training in mathematics (537bc). This is accomplished in order to accustom them to the study of permanent, immutable objects, and in this way, to prepare them for the study of the forms. Yet at the outset of *Republic* VIII, Plato has Socrates present a case where two different mathematical resolutions of a single questions are each legitimate. One way of calculating results in a human "harmony," the other way, a divine "harmony" (and a divine harmony will reliably produce divine offspring, i.e., philosophers [546ab]). Reeve maintains that the rulers "are able to calculate the Muses' geometrical number—certainly nothing in the story suggests that they cannot."[28] The problem is that we cannot tell which harmony is which. (The double aspect here is mirrored in the fact that the text suggests two distinct ways to calculate the nuptial number, either $2,700 \times 4,800$ or $3,600^2$). In the effort to breed philosophers to be in charge of the kallipolis, we may on occasion produce instead timocrats, who appear to love wisdom but who in fact love honor.[29] In this way, then, the kallipolis declines over time. Because mathematics is notoriously determinate, Plato is trying to show us that some decisions are *necessarily* indeterminate. In some cases, all one can do is to toss a coin. At *Critias* 115d, the city is initially laid out according to a perfect circular plan, but the demands of increasing commerce encourage the rulers to build straight roads and bridges into the city center. Although the rulers do the rational thing in this case, the roads and bridges upset the perfect circular plan, and the city begins to disintegrate. The cosmic analogue is the errant cause, *viz.*, whatever resists intelligent purpose. The errant case is chance or spontaneity (*Timaeus* 48a). For this reason, Cornford writes, the initial cosmic stuff, which is in "irregular motion" owing to the action of the errant cause (48a), must be "persuaded"—"because it is not wholly under [the] control" of Divine Reason.[30] Plato appears to recognize that "the best-laid schemes o' mice an' men gang aft agley," for example, that we can try everything in our power to do things in just the right way, but there is, both politically and cosmically, something utterly dark and in-illuminable by reason.[31] The kallipolis might come about by a combination of luck and divine intervention (*Republic* 499bd and 540d), but even if it did arise, it would not last. Our luck is bound to run out eventually. Meanwhile, we can "build the city" in our own souls, but even here, luck plays a role. Socrates is blessed by the occasional intervention of the daimonion, but the phenomenon, he testifies, is rare (*Apology* 31d).[32] Because there is, at the heart of the kallipolis (as well as at the heart of the cosmos, and at the heart of the individual agent) something impenetrably dark, because the fine city, if it comes about at all, only comes about by luck and divine intervention, and even then, it does not survive, the view that Plato's Socrates is intellectualist is vastly oversimplified. Socrates in fact recognizes that luck, both good and bad luck, plays a significant role in our live, in our cities and indeed, in our universe.

The divided line of *Republic* 508e ff. features, on one side, various epistemic states, and, on the other, their proper objects. The proper object of the imagination, naturally enough, is images. The next item on the epistemic ladder is *pistis*, trust, and its proper objects are sensible particulars. After this, the next epistemic function is *dianoia*, analysis, and its proper objects are mathematicals. The highest epistemic function is *epistemē*, knowledge, and its proper object is the system of the forms. As I understand the divided line image, however, these epistemic functions can apply to objects *other than* their proper objects. For example, one can have a false belief about a form. One can think that justice is the advantage of the stronger. If we agree that Thrasymachus is wrong about justice, he has an analysis of justice, but it is a false analysis. Yet his analysis is an analysis of *the form of justice*. A bad portrait of Jones is still a portrait of Jones. And so for the other epistemic functions: the proper object of an epistemic function is not its *only* object.

What I find astounding in the description of the line is the mathematical precision of its casting.[33] The length of the line segment representing imagination is exactly *twice* the length of line segment representing trust. Does this mean that it is *exactly* twice as easy to acquire a belief vià images as it is to acquire a belief vià sense perception?—Not 1.9 times as easy, but exactly 2.0 times as easy? The mathematical precision strikes me as out of place.[34] And we can compare this oddity to the mathematics of *Republic* VIII, already covered in this monograph. One "harmony" between spouses is divine, and the other "harmony" is human, but both "harmonies" follow the directions of the Muses. There is a right answer, but we cannot tell which answer is right. If we select the potential mates between whom exists the divine harmony, it is a matter of *luck*.

If the kallipolis comes into being, it is in part because of divine intervention. The nuptial number is 12,960,000, the number of days in a Great Year, when all the stars line up.[35] The suggestion that the stars, which are identified at *Timaeus* 39e as "heavenly gods," must be in alignment for the realization of the kallipolis to occur, again suggests that the gods are smiling on the world when kallipolis is actualized. And they smile on the world, evidently, only for a limited time.

In these cases, then—the unexplained precision of the divided line, the "harmonies" in breeding decisions, and the nuptial number itself—we find a remarkable mysticism about numbers. Even in mathematics, the paradigm of precision, Plato suggests that there is an element of uncertainty. Mathematics is not to blame for this, however: the culprit is human cognitive capacity.[36] Presumably, for example, the gods can tell which harmony in marriage is divine, and which is human—divine beings can tell when a harmony is divine, surely!—so there is a right answer, and that right answer is knowable—just not by us mere human beings. Plato's evident depression about human cognitive capacity explains the role of *luck*, both good and bad luck, not only in kallipolis but also in the good individual life. Insofar as living a life of perfect justice *does* depend on luck, it appears that virtue (or anyhow, the virtue of justice) cannot be taught. Again, Plato appears in this light to be non-intellectualist.

Moreover, as a writer, Plato uses not only rational argument, but also non-forensic techniques of persuasion. This aspect of his work seems distinctively non-intellectualist. Plato's Socrates is notorious for his wicked irony, as when he compliments Thrasymachus on his wisdom (*Republic* 337a). And Plato often names characters tellingly. "Meno" means "remainder," and Meno's mind is filled with other people's wisdom. He is the remainder left behind by now-dead famous men of the past. "Callicles" means "fine name or reputation;" Callicles quits the discussion to avoid admitting defeat (*Gorgias* 505d). "Polemarchus" means "first in war;" the character in *Republic* who gets all the trouble started by sending his slave chasing after Socrates to physically restrain him is named "Polemarchus." Socrates makes much of the fact that "Meletus" means "he who cares;" he says several times in *Apology* that Meletus does not care at all ("You have never had any care for our young people" [25c]; "Jurymen, Meletus does not care about any of these things" [26b]; etc.). "Thrasymachus" is pretty close of *thrasymē machē*, "over-confidence in battle." Polus' name is widely thought intended to call to mind *pōlos*, "colt," as he is young and frisky;[37] it may also call to mind "*polus*," the singular of "*poloi*," *the Many*, as he is a spokesperson for *the Many*. Thus, Polus is frisky and young Mr. Many. These plays on words give us further instances of Plato's use of non-forensic elements in his effort to win us over.

Other literary features are present in Plato's prose as well. The first word of *Republic* is *katabēn*, "I went down." This is echoed when Glaucon tells the Gyges' ring story. The unjust shepherd also "goes down" to rob a grave (359d6). And again, when Socrates relates the cave-conceit, the philosopher, who has been outside and seen real things, feels pity for the prisoners down below, who are playing their shadow-games, and so he, too, "goes down" (516e4). The same verb appears in all these places.[38] These literary touches help to unify the dialogue, and exhibit appeals to the extra-rational—the appeal is not just to the head, but also to the heart. The sense of beauty, and the appreciation of harmony and symmetry, help to win us over.

Rational persuasion *and* extra-rational influences each play a significant role in Plato's philosophical writing. The story that Plato wrote a tragedy, then, after he encountered Socrates, burned it, may well be apocryphal,[39] but it is the sort of story that *should have been true*, even if it is not. Plato surely is, and must be aware that he is, a writer of considerable skill. As much as he struggles against rhetoric and sophistry in his early work, he seems to acknowledge his own use of rhetorical techniques when he countenances philosophical rhetoric in the *Phaedrus* (259–62).[40] Plato is not, I think, strictly or exclusively intellectualist. The road to Larissa case at *Meno* 97a shows that virtue does not require knowledge, while the statues of Daedalus case (97d–98a) shows that knowledge is preferable to mere belief, even to true belief, since knowledge is more stable. But the position that we can be fully virtuous based only on true beliefs is distinctively non-intellectualist. An instance of virtue without philosophical reflection appears in that fact that the auxiliaries of the *Republic* are courageous but have only true beliefs (not knowledge) of the things that are truly to be feared (*Republic* 429ad).[41]

My thesis in all this has been that Plato takes the unity of the virtues to be crucial for us to apprehend, but that his apparent attempts to establish unity are actually indirect, dialectical demonstrations of its ineffability. That this thesis seems to be incompatible with the scholarly orthodoxy concerning intellectualism does not, then, disturb me, since I maintain that Plato's work, as well as Plato's Socrates, are not strictly intellectualist. That Plato's Socrates heeds dreams and oracles (*Apology* 33c), that he obeys the promptings of the daimonion, that Plato thinks certain kinds of harmony and certain melodies shape the soul (*Republic* 522ab)—all suggest Plato's acknowledgement of certain extra-rational influences on human life.[42]

If I know what is good and what is bad for me, I will do things conducive to my benefit and I will avoid doing things that are harmful to me. When I do things that are harmful to me, it is because I do not understand what I am doing. An unjust tyrant does things that are bad for himself. Even though he thinks he is doing just what he wants, he really is not doing so, since he wants what is good for him but he does not know what is good for him (*Gorgias* 466a–468e).

Still, it is not quite right to hold that virtue is knowledge.[43] It would be better to say that knowledge is virtue. If I know that cowardice is destructive of my soul, then I will not behave in a cowardly fashion. If I understand what courage is, I will be courageous, but I can be courageous (by a kind of instinct) without knowing what courage is. Socrates is brave—the way he faces his execution shows this. And Laches also testifies about Socrates' bravery on the battlefield (*Laches* 181ab). Yet Socrates denies knowing what courage is. He would say, I think, that he does not know whether he is courageous or not, since he does not know what courage is. So knowledge implies virtue, but virtue does not imply knowledge. One can, for example, be temperate by nature *(Charmides* 157–8). Just as Socrates, Lysis, Menexenus and Hippothales may *be* friends, although they do not know what friendship is (*Lysis* 223b)—they may be friends, but they don't know whether they are—so Socrates may *be* courageous without knowing what courage is, and, hence, without knowing that he is courageous.

So, if I know what is good for me and what is bad for me, I will behave rightly. But it is not quite right to say that virtue *reduces to* knowing what is good and bad for me. Doing what is good for me does not require knowing what is good for me. In the *Laches*, Socrates moves from, "Courage is wisdom about future goods and evils," to "Courage is wisdom about good and evil."

Then he complains that wisdom about good and evil seems to be a characterization of all virtue, not just of courage. Several scholars have taken this at face value, concluding that virtue is knowledge of good and evil.[44] But while such knowledge does guarantee virtuous behavior, virtuous behavior is possible without such knowledge. Again, Socrates himself is a courageous person, but he would be the first to admit that he does not *know* (in the strict Socratic sense of that word) what courage is, let alone the good for humanity.

A further complication is that one's choices in life might well reveal an understanding of what is really valuable (and what is not), but such wisdom, which we may call wisdom-in-behavior, does not require theoretical wisdom. Vlastos testifies that the bravest man he ever met would have flunked an elenctic examination on the nature of courage.[45] But still, doubtless, that man's choices showed that he understood what is truly valuable and what is not. Laches says that he knows what courage is, that he recognizes it when he sees it, but it keeps eluding his grasp whenever he reaches for it (*Laches* 194ab). I think Plato feels considerable sympathy for him here. One need not have a fully worked-out theory of virtue in order to understand intuitively what courage is. The soldier who sacrifices himself, smothering a grenade with his body, shows *behaviorally* that he understands courage, even if, prior to his demise, he could not have offered a philosophically satisfying definition of "courage."

Still, "what we know, we must be able to explain to others," Socrates maintains at *Laches* 190c. And at *Charmides* 159a, he tells Charmides, "Since you *have temperance* within *you, you* must hold *an* opinion about it. For [temperance] being in *you,* I presume it *must* . . . afford *some* perception of itself. . . ." But if unity is essential to virtue and if unity is ineffable, then virtue cannot, strictly speaking, be known discursively. If we cannot explain something, then we do not know it. A true belief without a *logos* is not knowledge. If it were straightforwardly true that virtue is knowledge, it would follow that no one is virtuous.

What I propose we do to relieve this tension is to construe the passages from *Charmides* and *Laches* somewhat loosely. Of course, it is *better* if we have discursive knowledge of the virtues, with definitions at the ready. But I take Socrates to be urging Charmides and Laches at these points in these dialogues not to give up.[46] He would not really maintain that one who cannot define "virtue" cannot be virtuous. Plato obviously thinks Socrates is virtuous, but Socrates says he knows "nothing at all about virtue" (*Meno* 80b). Since a necessary feature of virtue is ineffable, no fully articulated definition of "virtue" is available. Yet there are virtuous people—notably, Socrates himself. They make courageous choices; they face their executions with nobility. They manifest their understanding of virtue behaviorally.

I have argued elsewhere that Plato thinks that, as philosophers, we both know and do not know what we are seeking. In the *Theaetetus*, Plato argues that we know what knowledge is, since we are prepared to distinguish cases of genuine knowledge from cases of ersatz knowledge, but we do not know knowledge in the sense that we have not succeeded in defining "knowledge."[47] It is the same, I think, for virtue. We know what it is, in that we recognize cases of it, and in that we characteristically make the right choices, but we do not know what it is in that we are not able to define it. No one is able to do so. Not even the gods.

If the gods have a conceptual system not unlike our own, then not even the gods can define "virtue," because the virtues' being both one and many transcends that language. And a situation in which the gods had a different linguistic or conceptual system, I think, would be intolerable from a religious point of view. For suppose the gods had a conceptual system different from our own. Then when Chairephon asked the oracle whether anyone is wiser than Socrates, the answer should have been, "It all depends on what you mean by 'wiser.'" As it is, the oracle answers in the negative, but this would not be *fair* if the gods mean something irrecoverably different than what we mean by "wiser." It might, indeed, require considerable work to uncover what the gods mean by "courage" or "wisdom," but it must be recoverable. Otherwise, the gods would be systematically *tricking* us. If the gods operate with a different conceptual system, it is hard to see how they can make demands on us, or understand our prayers.

The upshot seems to be that the gods must, after all, speak our language. And thus, not even the gods have (discursive) knowledge of virtue, because of the unity/diversity conundrum. But the gods might still manifest behaviorally an understanding of virtue,[48] even though they, like us, cannot seem to define it. So it would still be true that Socrates' (early Plato's) gods are fully moral.

Chapter Eight

Indirect Argument in Plato

In a two-value logic system, a proof that an argument is valid may be conducted directly, by drawing legitimate inferences sanctioned by the rules from the premises. But a proof may also be conducted indirectly. An indirect proof assumes the premises to be true and the conclusion to be false. The proof then derives a contradiction from these assumptions, from which it follows that it is impossible for the premises to be true while the conclusion is false, or, in other words, that the argument is valid. The offspring of indirect proof is the *reductio ad absurdum*, where we assume the contradictory of the proposition we want to prove, then we show that that assumption has absurd and thus unacceptable consequences. If that assumption is false, our thesis is true.

The *locus classicus* of indirect argument would be Xeno's arguments in support of Par-menides. Xeno argues that, if space and time are divisible, they are infinitely divisible, and if they are infinitely divisible, then motion is impossible. Motion is obviously *not* impossible, so time and space must not be divisible at all.[1] Plato picks up this kind of argument at *Sophist* 244b, maintaining that the consequence of maintaining that there is only unity is that it is false that there is only unity.

Plato seems to think that some parts of his doctrine are best shown to be right indirectly. A reading of *Parmenides* illustrates this strategy. Parmenides warns Socrates that he must posit a theory of forms ("the one," in the language of the dialogue), for, if he does not, he will thereby "utterly destroy the power of language and of thought" (135bc). This is itself an indirect argument. Language and thought obviously are real, and these facts are incompatible with the claim that there are no forms. Therefore, there are forms. But to make it historically possible that Socrates actually spoke to Parmenides, Parmenides would have had to have been very old and Socrates very young—

a teenager, in fact.² Allen and Miller³ understand Plato to be saying, "You must have theory of forms, on pain of destroying thought and discourse. Just avoid positing an *adolescent* theory of forms, like the theory of this young fellow." He shows us *indirectly* what errors we need to avoid by parading the consequences of making those very errors. And again, in a case already cited, the Socrates of the *Meno* shows that virtue is not taught, nor is it innate. Meno himself is perplexed at this point. "How do good people arise or come to be (*gignomenōn*) at all?" he asks (96d). Answering this objection, Socrates posits divine inspiration, like the inspiration received by poets and prophets (99de), who say many useful things, but without understanding what they are saying (95bc, 97b). The gods have blessed good people with sound intuitions, since many people who are clearly good people themselves cannot, it seems, offer philosophically satisfying accounts of virtue.⁴

Now then, the claim that people become good by divine intervention may embody a metaphor.⁵ In line with this understanding, we may possess these things *as though* by divine dispensation. By likening the acquisition of virtue to poetic inspiration, Plato suggests that we can learn things we were not taught.⁶ But he does not argue for the claim, because doing so would require spelling out a full account of the nature of education and indeed, would require positing a full philosophy of mind. And the Socrates Plato represents in *Meno* backs away even from the reincarnation story he himself earlier related—he refuses even to "confidently assert" the story to be true (86b). *This* Socrates could not consistently offer a comprehensive philosophy of mind. He tries to *show* that learning without having been taught is possible with the slave boy episode, but he does not argue for the point. Again, some things must be *seen*.

Plato in these cases arguably lets us know what he is thinking *indirectly*. If so, it is not implausible to maintain that Plato also represents the ineffability of the unity of the virtues indirectly. Admittedly, there is no direct argument that unity is ineffable. The explanation of this fact that I offer is that such an argument would require a theory of what cannot be said, and such a theory seems to be in danger of being caught in its own echo. As we cannot seem to give an account of giving an account, or offer a truth about all truths, so we cannot seem to say what cannot be said. And aside from this consideration, it certainly would be *well beyond* the early Socrates, whom Vlastos calls Socrates$_E$,⁷ ("E" for "early") to float a full-blown theory of meaning. Instead of a direct argument, Plato has Early Socrates, Socrates$_E$, *suggest* ineffability. He allows poems, songs and stories to enter the discussion, and this shows that elements other than mere arguments are relevant. Just as Simonides can criticize Pitacus without having a full theory of the good, so too, Socrates can criticize Protagoras without having a full theory of virtue. Since (as I claim) an essential part of virtue is ineffable, we must "see" that part of it—we cannot argue for it. We cannot even state it properly. For these reasons, Socrates cannot bring out a full theory of virtue. This explains why Plato, even in his middle phase, and even though he does define the cardinal *virtues*, never even attempts a definition of "virtue."[8] In the *Protagoras*, both Socrates and Protagoras fumble over words; neither seems to be able to identify the bone of contention between them. Socrates also suggests arguments which he abandons in midstream, and this suggests that argument is nearing its limit. Two analogies for unity are suggested, but what I have argued, at any rate, is that neither is adequate for the task. Elsewhere in his corpus, Plato argues dialectically or indirectly, and he indicates that some matters are, in his judgment, beyond anyone's capacity to articulate. Finally, the arguments for unity are uniformly terrible arguments. It is possible, of course, that Plato suffered a major but temporary logical lapse, but a principle of charity would have us rather posit a reason why the unity arguments are so unpersuasive. Again, if the unity thesis cannot even be stated, it is not surprising that it cannot be argued for. It must finally be *seen* to be right.

As to what it means to say the virtues are one but many, suppose that Corporal Jones throws his body onto a live grenade, sacrificing his life to save the lives of the other soldiers in his unit. In doing this, Jones manifests great courage. It would be wrong to say that, in so acting, Jones exhibited piety.[9] Piety and courage are thus "not quite unconnected, but not the way you think, either" (331e), in other words, not just the same. Things can be unified without being identical, but we cannot quite articulate what this comes to. The virtues seem to be distinct in *Republic*, since each social station has its own dominant virtue. Rulers are wise, soldiers are courageous, and artisans are temperate. If virtue-words are names for the same state of soul, if temperance really is courage, we could just as well say that artisans are essentially courageous and soldiers, essentially temperate. Still, to be sure, soldiers in the kallipolis *are* temperate, but their dominant, kind-making virtue is courage. It would be wrong to say that the soldiers in kallipolis have as their dominant virtue temperance. Yet one of Socrates' examples of courage at *Laches* 191de is that of resisting a very strong desire, and this seems to assimilate courage with temperance. The virtues are "not quite unconnected, but not the way [Socrates] thinks, either."

In the introduction, I suggested the case of a man who borrows money, promises to repay it, but recognizes that he has a record of dishonesty, and this time, vows to a god that he will honor his debt. In this case, I argued, repaying the loan does manifest piety—thanks to the vow to the god—and it also manifests justice, but in an ordinary case, where there is no vow to a god in the offing, repaying a loan manifests justice, but not piety. I maintained in that chapter that the action of repayment does not, of course, thereby manifest impiety. It is just that piety or impiety do not arise at all—in the ordinary case. Let us now modify the case of Jones, the soldier who sacrifices his own life to save the lives of his comrades. Jones' action might have been piously motivated, but the action is clearly courageous.

Let us contrast two cases. 1) Jones throws himself on a live grenade, motivated solely by a desire to save the lives of others in his unit. 2) At T_1, Jones recognizes that he has, in the past, shown a tendency to avoid danger, and so he now vows to a god that the next time he is faced with danger, he will not back down. At T_2, Jones finds himself in dire straits, and this time, he does not seek to avoid danger, hurling himself on a live grenade. In case 2), Jones' action manifests both piety and courage, but in case 1), his action manifests just courage. And this shows that the attempt by some scholars to collapse the virtues must be mistaken. The virtues are not entirely separable, but they are not identical to one another, either. "Not this way, but not the way you think, either."

We speak of "showing great courage," but we do not speak of "showing great piety" or "showing great temperance." But when Charmides' robe accidentally (?) flies open at *Charmides* 155de, Socrates is apparently tempted to seize him. But Socrates does not act on the impulse, and we may say that he shows herein "great restraint." Still, we do not speak about "great temperance," and we certainly do not speak about "great piety." We feel entirely comfortable, however, with saying that the soldier shows great courage. So, restraint and courage, evidently, can be great, but not piety or temperance. And possibly this is because we recognize how easily we are tempted to indulge ourselves or to flee (respectively). Great discipline is required for us to overcome temptation in these cases.[10] Some virtues readily admit the predicate "great," while others do not, and this shows, again, that the virtues are non-identical.

Plato, then, occasionally indulges himself in indirect argument, and sometimes, in such arguments complicated by irony, as when he has Socrates characterize the middle books of *Republic* as a "digression" (*Republic* 543c). But Plato himself is remarkably indirect. He never appears in one of his dialogues; he is mentioned a few times, but only briefly.[11] And he is identified through the corpus as the author of dialogues, but by way of what is, apparently, a pseudonym.[12] So we have an author who hides behind the veil of a pseudonym, who never appears as a character in any of his dialogues, who forces his readers to think through what his actual beliefs are. Heraclitus writes "Nature loves to hide" (B 123). So does Plato!

Chapter Nine

The Importance of Unity

Philosophical ethics tends to be either action-focused or character-focused. The ethics of action posits various principles of action (*Keep your promises, Pay your debts*), and these principles tend to be anchored by some super-principle. The super-principle of utilitarianism is the Greatest Happiness Principle; the super-principle of Kantian deontology is the Categorical Imperative. Actions are justified by appeal to principles of action, and principles of action are justified by appeal to the super-principle.[1] The focus of action-ethics is, *What is the right thing for me to do?* The ethics of character, on the other hand, maintains that the emphasis of ethics is not on *What should I do?* but rather, the emphasis is on *What sort of person I should be or become?* Thus, Aristotle distinguishes between the continent agent and the virtuous agent (*Nicomachean Ethics* 1166b5–29). The continent agent has bad desires and resists them. But the virtuous agent has only good desires. Once you are good, you can do whatever you desire, since your desires will naturally be good. It is not that doing the right thing is unimportant, but if I succeed in fully inculcating the virtues into my character, then *of course,* I will do the right thing.

Ancient Greek ethics is fundamentally a character—rather than an action-ethics. What it is to be a good person and how one improves one's character are the central issues for ancient Greek moral philosophers. But the virtues can at times seem to conflict one with another. Suppose a child shows me a drawing she has just completed and asks me if I like it. Should I be honest? Or should I be compassionate? The virtues of honesty and compassion seem to be in conflict in this situation. Yet it is crucial for the ethics of character that a fully coherent moral life be possible, and that its possibility not hang on some *principle* of decision. (A hybrid philosopher could, of course, adopt the principle that in cases of conflict, justice favors compassion over honesty.

The addition of the principle would resolve the tension, but the ethics would no longer be pure virtue ethics.) Recognizing that different virtues can seem, at times, to recommend incompatible courses of action, virtue theorists typically posit a moral hero, a person in whom all the virtues operate at full strength. Plato posits the Philosopher-Ruler (*Republic* V, 471c ff.); Aristotle, the Great-Souled Man (*Nicomachean Ethics*, 1125^a); Confucius posits the Gentleman (*Analects*, 4.6, 6.20, 8.7); and Mencius, the Sage-King (*Mencius* IVA). The moral hero is intended in all these ethics-of-character theories to show that the fully moral life is attainable, and that it is attainable without appeal to any principles of action.[2]

And one might assemble further arguments to bolster the case for character-ethics. One might argue, for example, that courage is noble, while cowardice is worthless. What is desirable is distinct from what we in fact desire, as Ross observes,[3] and noble things are (really) desirable, while ignoble things are (really) worthless. If my friendly amendment to Plato is accepted, then temperance emerges as wisdom about what is (really) desirable. Part of what is really desirable is courage. From this it follows that temperance requires courage. There could be no temperate cowards. And this point is further supported by *Laches* 191de, where Socrates maintains that one can manifest courage in resisting a very strong desire. *Pace* Penner, however, this does not show that courage *is* temperance. It does not show that courage *reduces to* temperance. But it does show that the two are intimately connected. Again, it does not show that they are the same, exactly, but it does show that they are not altogether separable. The virtues are the same and they are different, and we cannot quite wrap our philosophical imaginations around how this can be so. Words fail us.

Again, if there are divine beings and if a right relationship with them is necessary for us to live the right kind of human lives—in a manner of speaking, *righteous* lives—then justice requires piety. There are no thoroughly just atheists. And *Euthyphro* 12e suggests that justice properly so-called concerns our relationships with other people, while piety concerns justice in relation to the gods. As already mentioned, one can be unjust to the gods. The Sibyl, who prays fervently for eternal life, was granted eternal life but not eternal youth, and she provides an instance. She eventually shrivels up and is imprisoned in an urn, which was stored in the temple as a warning against hubristic prayer.[4]

Piety and justice are closely connected, not the same but not different, either. Everything is like death—only different! At any rate, Plato might have argued in the ways indicated to link temperance with courage and piety with justice, and, doubtless, to link the other virtues as well. But he does not do so. It seems easy to conceive of an unjust, unreflective but brave soldier, and Plato's struggle against the separability this common intuition implies is drawn out much further than his claim of connection between piety and justice, just because the claim of connection between courage and wisdom is counter intuitive.

In the *Protagoras*, Plato represents virtue as an organic, homogenous whole, but he also recognizes that virtue has parts. How can virtue be both one and many? He tries by means of argument to establish unity by arguing that temperance is wisdom, and that piety is justice, but he finally only *gestures* in the direction of full unity. How exactly are they one? How can they be many *and* one? If they are one, why do we have different names for them?[5] We have become comfortable, Plato writes at *Cratylus* 403–4, referring to the gods as "Apollo," "Athena," "Zeus," etc., but we do not know their *real* names, the names they use to refer to each other. The real names of the gods are hidden from us, so we must our rough-and-ready nomenclature. But we should recognize that the names we use are partial, incomplete, and false. Just so, the actual virtues may be one and many, and our language obfuscates their interrelations.

After the *Protagoras*, he apparently abandons the project of trying to demonstrate unity. And in the *Protagoras* itself,

- the poor quality of arguments for unity;
- the fact that the unity thesis is at times fudged (the virtues are the same, or much the same, or at least they are not unrelated);
- the fact that some arguments are dropped altogether, abandoned before they are completed;
- the way Plato resorts to stories and metaphors;
- the fact that Plato apparently thinks that he not only cannot argue for but also cannot seem to *state* the thesis;
- the fact that the stage-setting in the *Protagoras* ubiquitously involves deception and hidden agendas;
- the fact that Plato does not ever revisit unity and that, after the *Meno*, he abandons altogether the project of defining "virtue;"
- the eventual claim that, rather than arguing for unity, we must rather come to "see" it—

all this, coupled with the necessity that, as a consistent ethics-of-character theorist, Plato must float *some* kind of a unity thesis,[6] supports my claim that the unity of the virtues, while it is essential to the real nature of virtue, is, in Plato's considered opinion, ineffable. Having abandoned the project of demonstrating unity/diversity, he eventually comes around to positing instead a moral hero in whom all of the virtues are fully instantiated.

If unity and diversity are crucial for us to apprehend but finally resistant to coherent articulation, then Protagoras, who claims to teach *whatever* his students lack, is a fraud. The wealthy Athenian we spoke of earlier, whose son has "just one problem"—that he is a coward—actually has a radically disordered soul. The boy does not need to spend his own time and his father's money with Protagoras "learning courage"—whatever that may entail! The boy is better off, as is Hippocrates at the outset, conversing with Socrates. But studying with Socrates will not consist in memorizing slogans. Meno tells Socrates that, if he really does not know what virtue is, he could have learned it from Gorgias (*Meno* 71c). (Gorgias bragged that he could answer any question. See *Gorgias* 449c). But the way to learn a virtue like courage, as well as the way to learn virtue, what-it-is, is by looking within. We must become, Vlastos admonishes us, our own teachers and our own students, because the answers we seek are already within us.[7] Socrates' interlocutors, as well as Plato's readers, cannot be spoon-fed. Meno, for example, has a terrific memory for what other people say,[8] but when you ask him what he thinks, his purse is pretty much empty. Yet even he knows what virtue is. If he had not a clue, asking him what virtue is would be a monumental waste of time.

None of this, of course, *proves* that Plato thinks that the unity of the virtues is ineffable. But Plato does not aim to analyze our conceptual system so much as he aims to reform it. That system features a gap where there should be something (we know not what!) filled in between "one" and "many" between "whole" and "part."

George Rudebusch has developed a criticism of Brickhouse and Smith and the similar construals of Clark, Woodruff and Ferejohn. Rusebusch lumps these together as "ambiguity interpretations." The general thesis is that Socrates uses "courage," "piety," "justice," and so on, in two distinct senses. One sense is when Socrates identifies virtue-words as referring to the same thing, "knowledge of what is good and bad for human beings."[9] These senses of the virtue-words surround "wholeness claims."[10] The essence of each virtue is the same, yet Socrates would surely claim not to possess anything so grand and sweeping as knowledge of the Good. He denies knowing what virtue is at *Apology* 19–20, *Laches* 186bc and 200e2–5, and *Meno* 71a. The other senses of virtue-words surround "partness claims." See *Laches* 197e, *Protagoras* 329c, and *Meno* 88a. There are, evidently, "parts" other than courage to virtue. The word play between these senses allegedly resolves the tension between wholeness and partness claims. When Socrates says that courage is a part of virtue, he means the deeds, not the power (the "essence") of virtue. When he says courage is the whole of virtue, he means the power ("the essence"), not the deeds, of courage.

It is possible, to be sure, that Plato suffers a temporary lapse in logic as he writes the *Protagoras*, but it certainly is noteworthy that Plato has Socrates come down hard on the young sophists in *Euthydemus* for their hiding behind equivocation. In that dialogue, I think, he shows that he regards arguments featuring equivocation fallacies as unworthy of serious philosophy.

According to Rudebusch, however, Socrates' real goal in the early dialogues is to convince Athenians that they are not nearly as wise as they think. The god's point ins saying no one is wiser than Socrates is that "Among humans, he is wisest who, like Socrates, recognizes that he truly has no valuable wisdom" (*Apology* 23b). One Socratic trick, according to Rudebusch, is to say something false, then see whether his interlocutor catches it. And so Socrates "makes the partness claim...as a way of testing" the wisdom of his interlocutors. Socrates himself "unequivocally accepts his arguments for the wholeness claim," writes Rudebusch, adding "as he ought to, seeing that they are compelling."[11]

I am not so sure. Is there a single study or discipline that concerns past, present and future goods and evils? Consider the study of history as a way of trying to avoid future errors. At a time of runaway inflation, an economist might caution that raising interest rates in order to provoke a recession does not always do away with inflation, citing what happened and what did not happen during the recession of 1969. The relevant discipline here is history, and history looks back. But it is invoked in order to formulate policy, and this is obviously forward-looking. Accurately describing the past is not the same discipline as predicting the future. The latter depends on the former, but they are not the same. I think Socrates is a little quick to posit a single discipline, as are the scholars who second him on the point.

But at any rate, Rudebusch thinks that when Socrates makes the "partness" claim, he does not mean it. A nimbler Protagoras would have denied that the virtues are separable. And it is undeniable that Socrates occasionally cites auxiliary premises in elenctic arguments that he himself does not endorse. For instance, he claims that the gods quarrel with each other at *Euthyphro* 6bc. But as to whether he himself believes the "partness" claim, however, I submit that he does. It would be wrong to say that in *Republic*, the kind-making virtue of soldiers is temperance, or that the kind-making virtue of artisans is courage. There are different kinds or "parts" of virtue. Socrates maintains that piety is to justice as odd is to number.

What Plato does present makes theoretical room for the thesis, and the thesis, if true, explains several otherwise anomalous features of the *Protagoras*. *Why are the arguments for unity so weak? Why does Plato abandon them?* And it also explains some ancillary puzzles, for example, *Why is "virtue" never defined anywhere in the corpus?* (He defines the virtues in *Republic*, but he never does define virtue itself.) And, *Why does Plato never return to arguing for unity?* Finally, it is true that the view that Plato holds that unity is real but ineffable flies in the face of scholarly orthodoxy concerning "Socratic intellectualism," but that hand, I have argued, has been substantially overplayed.

I have tried to show that other scholars' attempts at cashing out the unity thesis are unsuccessful, and I have argued that the reason why they fail is finally that the virtues are unified, but that the way in which they are unified—unified yet diverse, identical yet separate—defies coherent expression.[12] The ineffability of their unity is not just an unfortunate feature of Attic Greek or contemporary English. We do not possess the *conceptual* wherewithal to express properly the view. It is crucial for us to apprehend that unity, yet that apprehension must be brought about in a non-logical way.[13] Still, if the virtues are profoundly one, then they can be embodied in a perfectly virtuous person. Thus, the compatibility of the virtues, their coherence, is indicated or suggested by way of Plato's sketch of his moral hero.

But it is significant that the Philosopher-Ruler is only *sketched*. We don't get to *know* this character in the way we do get to know some of Plato's characters in his other dialogues. Meno has a personality, a style, if you will, and so does Euthyphro. But not the Philosopher-Ruler, and indeed, not the Eleatic Stranger, either. These two are stick-figures more than they are people. The philosopher-ruler embodies the elusive unity of the virtues; the Eleatic Stranger is a spokesperson for *nous*. They serve a strictly logical function; this is why they lack any personal characteristics. The halting articulation of the unity of the virtues thesis that we find in the *Protagoras* finally only *gestures* towards the coherence of the virtues, while the philosopher ruler of *Republic*, flat and two-dimensional though he is, *embodies* that coherence. Still, the doctrine cannot be properly argued for or even properly stated.

Conclusion

Plato thinks that some things are beyond the boundary of the *logos*. He elsewhere indicates a certain nervousness about giving an account of giving an account. He refuses to give an account of the Form of the Good, because, given a hierarchical theory of justification, there can be no justification of the *highest* of things. Similar nervousness explains why he never attempts to speak the truth about truth. He seems to think that some things are real but ineffable. It is my view that the unity of the virtues is, in Plato's considered judgment, such an issue. As we saw with the early Wittgenstein, any attempt to name what cannot be named is doomed to failure. And Plato himself ties meaning to naming in *Crarylus*, so it is not too great a stretch to suppose that, since it cannot be named (or, in other words, *identified*), the unity thesis cannot be stated. The best one can do in this situation is to *gesture* towards the ineffability of the target phenomenon. This explains why Plato resorts in the *Protagoras* to "poems and songs, pipings and dancing and harping" (348a). When Socrates demands to know whether Protagoras thinks the virtues are only slightly related, he answers, "Not quite that, but not in the way you believe, either" (331e–332a). Ironically, Protagoras speaks for Plato here. This is a further gesture towards ineffability. The truth of the matter remains elusive— *Not this way, but not that way either. . . .* One wants to ask, *Well, then, what way?* But the text provides no clear answer to this question. If the unity thesis really *cannot* properly be stated, such vagueness is not just tolerable but also necessary. And the unity arguments are not only inconclusive but also, they are uniformly terrible arguments, and one of them is utterly abandoned, and this suggests that Plato recognizes that, as arguments, they are weak. The arguments do not come close to establishing unity, but they do show the virtues to be in close connection to each other: Either $a=b$, or *a is like b*, or *a is at least not irrelevant to b*. For instance, one cannot be fully wise if one is intemperate, but this does not show that temperance = wisdom. Some scholars maintain that Plato deliberately inserts bad arguments in the dialogue to expose Protagoras, who, "although he claims to teach virtue, does not know what virtue is."[1] Some have held that "unity" is ambiguous between a psychological claim and a conceptual claim.[2] The majority of scholars think that Socrates prefers the lump of gold to the parts of a face for a unity-analogue. But both analogies Socrates suggests for unity, the parts-of-the-face analogy *and* the gold analogy, arguably are weak representations of the target-phenomenon. Our tendency as scholars is therefore to substitute analogies we find more congenial—different uses for the *technē* of triangulation, different hemispheres of the world, renamed cities, different species of a single genus, different individuals all being persons, partners in a marriage, etc. But none of these alternatives maps very well onto the target phenomenon. Thus, Plato may, after all, be right—perhaps the virtues are really profoundly one and yet undeniably diverse, and their peculiar status may indeed defy coherent expression. Plato, at any rate, never again takes up an argument for the unity of the virtues. In *Laws*, he only says we must try to "see" the unity of the virtues, but he makes no further attempts after *Protagoras* to argue for it or even to state it.

We have examined several explanations of the poor quality of the unity arguments in the *Protagoras*. One scholar thinks that the Plato who produced the dialogue is a philosophical neophyte, who has not yet mastered logical terminology. On this view, the arguments *are* weak, but Plato does not know it. But Protagoras' long speech is universally allowed to be a masterpiece of philosophical prose. This does not harmonize well with the claim that Plato is an immature writer at this point in time. Others have suggested that Plato is aware of the weakness of the arguments, and have claimed that, in representing Protagoras' failure to protest against Socratic sophistry, Plato is indirectly criticizing Protagoras. On this showing, Plato would be saying to himself, "I will show Protagoras to be intellectually bankrupt by having him fail to object to Socrates' obviously fallacious argument." This interpretation draws too much from silence. Another construal would be that Plato is belittling Socrates, putting arguments into his mouth that he, Plato, knows are non-starters. Some scholars have represented the low quality of the arguments as utterly dark and unfathomable. *My* Plato says to himself, "I will show the topic to be hopelessly obscure, indeed, ineffable, by having Socrates argue falteringly and fallaciously, fumbling even to articulate his thesis. There are things that are right and profound, but some of these things are beyond the scope of the logos." We are free *and* we are predestined; every word I have written is meaningless, yet meaningful; the virtues are one *and* they are many. Things that transcend language and logic must finally be *experienced*.

... John Wisdom tells the story of a certain Mr. Flood, a breeder of many lion cubs, who never lost one. "Asked the secret of his success, Mr. Flood replied, 'Understanding lions.' Asked of what consists in the understanding of lions, he replied, 'Every lion is different.' It is not to be thought," Wisdom continues, "that Mr. Flood, in seeking to understand an individual lion, did not bring to bear his great experience with other lions. Only he remained free to see each lion for itself."[3] To see the unity of the virtues, we must understand them, and understanding them will in part consist in recognizing their community, and in part, it will involve recognizing their distinctiveness one from another. The virtues are many *and* they are one, and our difficulty in coming to terms with this thesis is a consequence of the poverty of the human conceptual system. Paradoxically, our conceptual system is complete enough to show us that the virtues are one and many, but sketchy enough to prevent us from fully understanding this.

Notes

PREFACE

1. *NE*, I, 6.
2. See Vlastos, 1983.

INTRODUCTION

1. See my 2002.
2. See my 1992.
3. See my 2011.
4. See chapter IV of my 2008.
5. Burnyeat, 1990, 21–2. On the same note, see also McDowell, 1973, 163–4 and Waterfield, 54 n. 3.
6. See my 2005.
7. See my 2006 and my 2013.
8. Vlastos, 1983, 30.
9. See my 2010.
10. See my 2011.
11. Plato thinks philosophy is essentially dialogic, and he expresses considerable hesitation about committing his settled views to paper, since something a reader reads cannot answer back. See especially *Phaedrus* 278cd. See also *Apology* 18d, where he complains that he must speak to the jury but with no one to answer back.
12. See my 2008, 71–111, where I argue that the kind of expertise most prominent in Plato's sights here is *moral* expertise.
13. See my 2010, 67–9 and my 2008, 204–5.
14. I take "being" here predicatively, not existentially. The form of justice is the "being-ness," the *ousia*, of justice, the *what-it-is*-to-be just. Beyond, then, the form

of justice and the form of piety, etc., there is the form of the good, which is beyond being-just and beyond being-pious; indeed, it is beyond being-anything else whatsoever. It is simply "beyond being."

15. *Laws* 963. We shall return many times to this promissory note.

16. Concerning this passage, see my 2008, 30–9.

17. Taylor thinks the unity argument is difficult and subtle, and Plato's audience needs a break. This is why he inserts the otherwise-irrelevant Simonides episode. See Taylor, 1956, 251. I will argue that the Simonides poem is philosophically relevant to the issues at hand. See 59 and ff.

18. And, incidentally, what would Socrates think if Protagoras were to appeal to a little god, a daimonion, who whispers in *his* ear?

19. Keith McPartland raised this question at a conference, "Socratic Ignorance and Socratic Wisdom," held at Oregon State University April 25, 2002. When McPartland raised the question, Penner replied that if someone described the action of the soldier as *pious*, what she said would be "true but weird."

20. This seems to me to be a false dilemma. There is room between "They are all one and the same" and "They are entirely separate." I think Plato wants us to recognize this, even if his Socrates evidently does not. We shall come back to this text many times in what follows.

21. Compare the missing middle ground between "I know virtue" and "I know nothing at all about virtue" at *Meno*.71a

22. There is a nice statement of the unity thesis at 443de. The just person "binds all of [the virtues] together, and from having been many, becomes entirely one, temperate and harmonious."

23. It seems to me that the natural thing for Plato to do at this point would be to say, "*Of course* their definitions are similar. They are the same thing." Penner, however, thinks that, although temperance and justice *are* the same (in the same way that water and H_2O *are* the same), still, the *definitions* of the *words designating them* are distinct. Unity is a thesis about things, not about words. Thus Penner. He will be allotted his day in court later.

24. I grant that at *Laws* 963, he assigns to the Nocturnal Council the task of *studying* the unity and diversity of the virtues, striving to see how they can be both one and many. But he does not argue for their unity here, and he seems to be still uncertain about how something can be both one and many. Charles Kahn thinks Plato resolves the unity/diversity dialectic in *Republic*, but Kahn does not tell us *how* he does so. See Kahn, in Werkmeister, 1976. Shorey also says that, on the basis of *Protagoras* alone, Plato does not expect us to conclude that virtue is knowledge. The dialogue is an invitation for us to "think further, in the direction of the *Republic*." See Shorey, 2015, 83. Shorey also provides no further indication of *how exactly* he thinks the issue is resolved in *Republic*.

25. Compare to Kant, who urges that God and the afterlife are things that we cannot know about, but that they are things that we can *hope for*. See Rohlf, 2018, 114 ff.

26. So "A fact is whatever is the case" (Wittgenstein, 1963, §2, 7) is, strictly speaking, meaningless. And so is "All facts are facts," which seems to be analytically true, but is meaningless on Wittgenstein's showing. Wittgenstein says as much

at 1963, §6.54, 151. In a letter to Russell, Wittgenstein says that "the main point" of his early theory is "what cannot be expressed by propositions—and, what comes to the same, what cannot be thought." Quoted in Anscombe, 1971, 161. Anscombe's chapter on mysticism (1971, 161–73) is quite useful.

27. Wittgenstein, 1963, 31 (§3.333).
28. Wittgenstein, 1963, 151 (§ 7). The same general desire, to say what cannot be said, to think what cannot be thought, may be the source of the "transcendental illusion" of Kant—e.g., out desire to assign a *cause* to the cosmos. See Kant, A297/B354, in Müller, 1966, 223–4.
29. Wittgenstein, 1963, 151 (§ 7).
30. Smith, 1991, 198,
31. Smith, 1991, 128.
32. Russell, 1958, 2–3.
33. 1 Corinthians, 13:12.
34. Augustine, 2007, *Sermones*, 43, 9.
35. See *Timeus* 29a. "If the cosmos is beautiful and its constructor good, he must have fixed his eye on the eternal . . . If otherwise, and this would be an *impious* supposition. . . ."
36. "To the crows!" [*ball' eis korakas*] was a popular Greek curse, roughly equivalent to "Be hanged!"—or worse! See my 2011, 125, and 159–60, n. 14 concerning this phrase. See also Liddell\ nd Scott, 1940, v. I, 980.
37. See *Meno* 95c. What Meno "particularly admires" about Gorgias is that he sneers at those who, like Protagoras, claim to teach virtue.
38. Meno holds that either we already know virtue or we don't. Socrates thinks that in a way we know it and in a way, we don't know it. The way in which we don't know it makes it worthwhile for us to look for it. He says at *Apology* 23ab that we are all ignorant from a god's point of view, so that an individual who, like Socrates, recognizes his own lack of real wisdom is thereby the wisest *of people*.
39. This is Plato's apparent relation to the Form the Form of the Good. If he has a true belief, he has a belief. By insisting that only knowledge is dignified enough to pair with the Form of the Good, Socrates does *not* avoid positing a belief about the Form of the Good. His refusal to discuss in a direct way the Form of the Good, I argue, may be a consequence of Plato's theory of explanation. See my 2010, 37–45.
40. The gods are wholly moral, and so it might seem that the gods would have the complete moral theory, since "virtue is knowledge." But if unity and diversity among the virtues are necessary features of the virtues, but features that cannot be articulated, then that theory cannot be coherently stated, even by the gods. Maybe the gods *have* the complete moral theory but cannot *state* it. Yet "what we know, we must be able to state" (*Charmides* 159). If the "we" here includes the gods, the gods must be able to state the theory—perhaps they can state it, but in a language we cannot understand!
41. Vlastos thinks Socrates engages in such word-play. Vlastos distinguishes know-ledge$_E$ from knowledge$_C$. Knowledge$_C$ is certain knowledge, while knowledge$_E$ is knowledge-elenctic. Knowledge$_E$ comes to "I know—but I could well be wrong." See Vlastos, 1983, 46. But this kind of "knowledge" sounds to me not like knowledge

at all, but rather, very firmly held belief. If I know it, it *must* be true. There is simply no room for "I know it but I could be wrong."

42. Kitching, 2003, 201.

43. They "wander around" between being and not-being;" a particular human being both is human, yet when he is drunk, he is scarcely human at all.

44. What he actually says here is "What is so wonderful [*thaumaston*] about [particulars being beset with problems]?" This word, "wonderful," comes from the same root of the word Plato uses when he says that philosophy begins *in wonder*. See *Theaetetus* 155c–d, where Theaetetus confesses that he is "lost in wonder" at Socrates' puzzles about being and becoming. Socrates answers, "The sense of wonder [*to thaumazein*, "the wondering"] is the mark of the philosopher. Philosophy indeed has no other origin." Trans. Cornford, 1957, 43. See also *Meno* 84c: the slave boy only begins to inquire when he begins *to wonder*. These passages from *Meno* and *Theaetetus* may well be the source of Aristotle's remark that "philosophy begins in wonder" at *Metaphysics*, I, 982b.

45. Brickhouse and Smith think that what Socrates denies is *knowing how*, as opposed to *knowing that*. He does know *that* virtue is beneficial to the virtuous person; he just does not know *how* this is true. See Brickhouse and Smith, 1994, 18–9. I should think that, especially given Socrates' rather restrictive conception of knowledge, if one does not know how virtue is beneficial to the virtuous person, one does not really know that it is so.

46. Socrates says art *Apology* 23ab that we are all ignorant from a god's point of view, so that someone who, like Socrates, recognizes his own lack of wisdom, is thereby wiser than those who only imagine that they know.

47. Trans. Reeve. 2004, 119.

48. Socrates says at its conclusion, "Why do we not say goodbye to songs and poems, and get back to what I first asked?" (347c). Many scholars take their cue from Socrates here. Beresford calls Socrates' analysis of the poem "pedantic." See Beresford, 2005, 150, n. 59. Vlastos calls the extended gloss of Simonides a "tongue-in-cheek digression;" see Vlastos, 1991, 136. Guthrie dismisses the passage as "splendid entertainment, but hardly philosophy." See Guthrie, 1986, IV, 227. Crombie thinks the episode shows that "you can make a poem mean anything you like. . . . Reliance on poetry . . . is misguided." Crombie, 1963, v. I, 234. Grube finds it to be illustration of the way Socrates can "out-sophisticate the sophists." Grube, 1980, 220. Frede takes it to be part of a "major interruption" in the dialogue, an interruption that is irrelevant to its overall argument. Frede, 1992, xxvii. I try to identify some philosophically compelling points arising out of the "Ode" below, 58–60.

49. Vlastos, 1983, 56. The phrase also comes up in Vlastos, unpublished

CHAPTER ONE

1. Translation of this passage from Lombardo and Bell, 1992, pp. 19–20.

2. The example is Frede's. See Frede, 1992, p. xxvii. I discuss Frede's analogy below, 37–8.

3. See Guthrie's commentary 1956, 33.
4. Guthrie, 1956, 35.
5. Guthrie, 1986, v. IV, 222.
6. See 20–22 on the *Laches'* (supposed) definition of "virtue entire."
7. Adam, 2013, ix.
8. Friedlander, 1958, v. I, 19. Guthrie writes that "men or actions are just," but that justice itself is not. Justice itself does not have "the characteristic" of justice. Guthrie, 1986, v. IV, 223. Vlastos maintains that, since no one wants to say justice is unjust, Plato thinks that justice must be just. This represents a false dilemma, Vlastos says. See Vlastos, 1981, 249, n. 76.

It might be observed against such dismissive construals that the arguments with more modest conclusions are less offensive, and maybe this is Plato's point. Temperance is wisdom, in whole or in part, or it is like wisdom, or at least it is not like foolishness. This suggests that in Plato's mind, both Socrates and Protagoras stake out extreme positions.

9. See Wakefield, 1991.
10. Taylor, 1998, 68–9 maintains that the theory is incoherent: virtue, on his showing, is represented as intrinsically good and as *only* instrumentally good.
11. See Allen 1970, 94–5.
12. Frede, 1992, xvii.
13. Frede, 1992, xxiii; Penner, 1992, 165; Cooper, 1999, 80; Brown in Beresford, 2005, xvi.
14. This premise, so far as I can tell, is false. "Foolish" has several different contraries, depending on the context of its use. *Wise, sly, intelligent, careful, scrupulous, crafty, clever, devious*—any of these can be the contrary of "foolish," depending on the context of its use, and it is just not true that whoever is intelligent is sly. When we say, "Nixon was no fool," we do not mean to imply thereby that Nixon was wise. And the logic of the individual virtues also differs. One can show great courage but not great temperance, perhaps because we recognize that courage is so hard to maintain. "Great piety" also seems *strained*—either you are pious or you are not, I should think. Still, one can show great impiety.
15. Rickless seems to make this error. The fact that courage is not identical to ignorant-confidence is taken to imply that courage is identical to knowing-confidence. See Rickless, 1998, 365.
16. See Guthrie, 1986, v. IV, 224.
17. See Frede, 1992, xxv. Frede observes that Plato, for one, regards self-predication as *obvious*. Any adequate account must show how the claim seems obvious to Plato. If an account represents the unity claim as absurd, then that account is mistaken. Thus Frede.
18. See below, 55–9.
19. See Vlastos, 1981, 237.
20. Grube thinks that Plato actually conflates the "is" of identity with the "is" of predict-ation here in *Protagoras*. See Grube, *Plato's Thought*, 220–1. But a principle of charity would suggest that, since he is aware of the difference in *Republic*, he is

aware of it also in *Protagoras*, and he sets out an argument here in the latter dialogue which he knows embodies an error. His point is dialectic (or so I will argue).

21. Keyt throws in the towel in his assessment of the uniqueness of the world argument in *Timaeus*, labeling the demiurge "mad." See Keyt, 1971. In general, the Straussians claim to have uncovered fallacies in Socrates' reasoning; they then conclude that Plato harbors dark motives for providing Socrates with terrible arguments which employ these fallacies. Bloom, for instance, thinks Plato is disparaging Socrates in *Republic*; the point of the exercise is to make us laugh at the very idea of Philosopher Rulers. See Bloom, 1991.

22. See Vlastos, 1981, 237. Wakefield argues that the fact that piety is like justice and vice versa does not entail that piety *is* justice. See Wakefield, 1991. Friedlander thinks the unity arguments in *Protagoras* aim to establish strict identity, but that they are deliberately fallacious. Friedlander's Plato inserts obviously fallacious arguments in the dialogue owing to an "iridescent irony, hard to grasp." Friendlander, 1958, v. 1, 19. Allen thinks he sees the motive for Plato using such unpersuasive arguments: he thinks "blatantly and scandalously fallacious" arguments will help to expose Protagoras, who, "although he claims to teach virtue, does not know what virtue is." See Allen 1970, 94–5. Frede also takes the low quality of the unity arguments to be a way of exposing Protagoras as a fraud (Frede, 1992, xvii). Other scholars see Plato's use of fallacious arguments as an *invitation* to his readers to work out the unity of the virtues for themselves: Frede (1992, xxiii); Penner (1992, 165), and Cooper (1999, 80). In this regard, see also Weiss, 2006. Perhaps he passes the baton on to future philosophers by assigning the task to the Nocturnal Council (*Laws* 963).

23. Penner, 1992; Frede 1992.

24. Frede, 1992, Cooper, 1999, Kahn, 1976, and Penner, 1992.

25. Woodruff, 1992. The virtues, Woodruff thinks, are one in essence, and that essence is knowledge of good and evil, but the virtues differ in their accidents, in "the things that are true of" them (104). Having a virtue requires having the essence of that virtue. It would follow that, since Socrates is courageous and temperate, he has the essence of courage and temperance, which is knowledge of good and evil. But Socrates would surely deny knowing good and evil. Kraut says that "knowledge of good and evil" is too vague to serve as a useful definition of "virtue"—it "fails to provide a useful standard for making practical decisions." See Kraut, 1984, 200.

Taylor also thinks the virtues are one and the same thing and that they are knowledge of what is best for the agent, applied to different areas of life. See Taylor, 1998, 67–8. Justice, again, does not fit the bill here.

26. Woodruff, 1992, 104. I am not so sure that *everything true* of an object is a property of that object, and for this reason, I am hesitant to grant that the accident of location is an accidental *property* of a ping pong ball. It may be true that x is larger than y, but being larger than y does not appear to me to be a property of x, but rather, a relation between x and y. Concerning "knowledge of good and evil" as *a definition* of "virtue," see below, 138 ff.

27. Taylor also thinks the virtues are "one and the same thing and that they are knowledge of what is best for the agent, applied to different areas of life." See Taylor, 1998, 67–8. Justice, again, does not fit the bill here.

28. In his paper "Was Polus Refuted?" Vlastos argues that, in the *Gorgias*, Socrates apparently thinks that if he can show that it is not the case that doing injustice is always better than suffering injustice, he will thereby have secured that suffering injustice is always better than doing it. But there is a third possibility: sometimes, one is better and sometimes, the other is better. Plato at this point in his career seems unaware of the difference between contraries and contradictories. See Vlastos, in Graham, 1995. Later in his career, Plato appeals to this very distinction in his argument against the notion that the good for humanity must be either intellectual pursuit or sensual pleasure. He now sees this is a false dilemma, claiming that the good for humanity involves both some physical pleasure and some intellectual pleasure. Since *Philebus* appears at the end of his career, Plato may well have been made aware of the difference between contradictories and contraries by Aristotle.

29. *Philosophical Investigations*, 261.

CHAPTER TWO

1. As Vlastos puts it in his 1981, 52–9. He is joined by Frede, 1992, x.

2. In his 1967, 454–5, Vlastos writes that sometimes, Plato's logic is "a little wobbly." I concur.

3. Vlastos maintained that "the bravest man I ever knew would have flunked an elenctic examination on the nature of courage." Quoted by Woodruff, 1992, 101. In the *Meno*, Socrates maintains that people who achieve great things without being terribly reflective—soldiers in battle, for example—are divine. They possess true opinions in a way "no different from. . . prophets and tellers of oracles, who under divine inspiration, utter many truths, but have no knowledge of what they are saying" (99c). According to this revised view, it seems that one could be brave without being wise. Yet one can, evidently, be temperate by nature (*Charmides* 157–8? isenoughto make us brave. it is more stable, but behevioral ehavior that she believws that some things are worse than d) and one can exhibit wisdom about what is genuinely to be feared without having done much moral philosophy. The brave solider shows *by her behavior* that she believes that some things are worse than death. Discursive wisdom is best, since it is more stable, but behaviorally manifested wisdom is enough to make us brave.

4. Socrates often complains when his interlocutors speechify, but he does so himself on occasion,

5. For better or worse, the Greek word for "courage," *andreia*, is derivative of *andr-*, the genitive root for *anēr*, man, in the sense of *adult male human being*. *Andreia* comes to *manliness*. For this reason, one occasionally finds Socrates saying "Be a man and answer," (*Gorgias* 494d), or referring to the "manly virtue" [*andros aretē*—*Protagoras* 325a2]. (Curious, however, that *andreia* is a feminine noun!)

6. Note that *Apology* makes it clear that Socrates has no fear of death (fear of death, he declares, is "the basest sort of ignorance"—29b), but he stubbornly refuses to damage his soul by doing anything unjust. If the jury were to instruct him to cease doing philosophy, he would refuse. See *Apology* 29cd. Vlastos maintains that "the

bravest man I ever met" would have "flunked an elenctic exam." (Quoted by Woodruff, 1992, 101.) In the *Meno*, it is asserted that people who achieve great things without being terribly reflective—soldiers in battle, for in-stance—are like prophets and oracles, "who under divine inspirations, utter many true things, "but have no knowledge of what they are saying." Under the revised view, however, it seems that one could be brave without being wise.

There has been much discussion of this passage in relation to its alleged inconsistency with Socrates' apparent resolution to do whatever the state demands at *Crito* 50e–51c. See especially Brickhouse and Smith, 1994, 143–9 and Kraut's extended study of the issue, 1984.) But the point to which I wish to draw attention is that Socrates is wise concerning what is truly dreadful (damage to his soul), and because he has this wisdom, he does not fear death, thus displaying his courage.

Ferejohn argues that piety may be represented as knowledge of what is good and bad for the gods. See Ferejohn, 1984. But according to the *Euthyphro*, we cannot do anything to improve the condition of the gods. The view that we benefit the gods by prayer and sacrifice is part of the "commercial" view of piety Socrates roundly rejects. See *Euthyphro* 13e–15a, esp. 14e.

7. This would disturb everybody but Penner, since unity, according to him, comes to strict identity, but unity is not a thesis about what we mean when we speak about courage. According to Penner, it would be true that wisdom about desire is courage, though we would not *say* this.

8. Trans. by Guthrie, 1986, 223. Emphasis my own.

9. Compare this to *Sophist* 251a, Plato maintains that motion and being can combine, but not so motion and rest. Some forms, he now sees, "interweave" and some do not.

10. A similar reading is offered by Savan, 1964.

11. See also Vlastos, 1981, 237.

12. Plato's logic has been criticized here. For example, Adam and Adam, 1905, ix allege that Plato identifies the non-just with the unjust. Guthrie, 1975, v. IV, 226 and Grube, 1980, 220 maintain that Plato fails to distinguish between the "is" of identity and the "is" of predication, though, they grant, he does later correct this error at *Sophist* 255cd. Guthrie finds self-predication ridiculous; he writes "Men have the characteristic, but justice *is* the characteristic" (Guthrie, 1975, v. IV, 223, n.2; cf. 222). Grube claims that Plato fails to distinguish contradictories from contraries (Grube, 1980, 220). Plato later, Grube might have noted, patches this up in the *Philebus*. In that dialogue, Plato comes to see that the view that the good for humanity is the life of physical pleasure is only the contrary, not the contradictory, of the view that the life of mental pleasure is the good for humanity, so the two do not exclude each other. Because *Philebus* is late, Plato's later logic might well have been sharpened by Aristotle. See Aristotle's *Categories* 10 for the distinction between contradictories and contraries. Brown seeks to excuse Plato for the "evident flaws" in his arguments, indicating that the dialogue is intended to be an "invitation to philosophy," rather than a settled expression of Plato's own views. See Brown, in Beresford, 2005, xvi.

13. See also *Hippias Major* 289ab and *Symposium* 211a.

14. This implicit understanding of self-predication will be seen to owe much to Nehamas' classic paper on self-predication. As Nehamas reads the theory of forms, particular F's "do not *deserve*" the title of "F." We may say that pious particulars are only "sort-of pious." See Nehamas,1979, 101. A similar view of self-predication can be found at Meinwald, 1992.

15. This understanding of the nature of virtue as a whole is advocated, so far as I understand them, by Brickhouse and Smith, 1996.

16. I find it disappointing that "temperance" is not defined as "wisdom about desire." This would be perfectly parallel to the definition pf "courage" as "wisdom about fear."

17. Plato also feels sympathy for Meno, I think, when Meno says that sometimes, he thinks the sophists teach virtue and sometimes, he does not (*Meno* 95c). Virtue can be learned but it cannot be (reliably) taught, and so it is not quite right to say either that the students of the sophists are taught virtue or that they do not learn it. Laches, too, says at one point, "I am really getting annoyed at being unable to express what I think . . . I still think I know what courage is, but I cannot understand how it has escaped me just now so that I cannot pin it down in words and say what it is" (*Laches* 194b). At *Charmides* 159a, however, Socrates maintains that, if someone really is temperate, that person will have "a sense of its presence, by way of which that person will form an opinion . . . of what sort [of thing] it is." This, I think, is what we should aim for—fully articulating what is present already inside us. But that it is elusive, I think, Plato grants, and I believe he feels some sympathy for Laches and, indeed, for Meno.

18. In *Philebus* and in *Sophist* Plato shows awareness of false dilemmas. See note 13.

19. There is almost universal agreement among scholars that the Simonides exegesis is a distraction. Socrates says at its conclusion, "Why do we not say goodbye to songs and poems, and get back to what I first asked?" (347c). Many scholars take their cue from Socrates here. Vlastos calls the extended gloss of Simonides a "tongue-in-cheek digression." See Vlastos, 1991, 136. Guthrie dismisses the passage as "splendid entertainment, but hardly philosophy." See Guthrie, 1986, IV, 227. Crombie thinks the episode shows that "you can make a poem mean anything you like. . . . Reliance on poetry . . . is misguided." See Crombie 1963, I, 234. Grube finds it to be illustration of the way Socrates can "out-sophisticate the sophists." See Grube, 1980, 220. Frede takes it to be part of a "major interruption" in the dialogue, an interruption that is irrelevant to its overall argument. See Frede, 1992, xxvii.

But the passage goes on for eight Stephanus pages, from 339 to 347, and it would be unlike Plato to engage in such a long digression without having *some* point in mind. As for Socrates apparently thinking that the exercise is a waste of time, it should be recalled that Plato has Socrates call the middle books of the *Republic* a "digression" (543c), and he does the same when it comes to the detailed contrast between philosophers and rhetoricians in the *Theaetetus* (177c). Yet the middle books of the former and the juxtaposition of philosopher and rhetorician in the latter are the very heart and soul of their respective dialogues. We should be cautious about agreeing too quickly with the dismissal of songs and poems in the *Protagoras*, as this may, after all, be ironic.

20. He says at *Apology* 23ab that we are all ignorant from a god's point of view, so that an individual who, like Socrates, recognizes his own lack of real wisdom is thereby the wisest of people. Concerning being unjust to ourselves, see Falk's classic treatment of the issue in Bloomfield, 2008.

21. When Meno says he cannot find one quality that all virtues have in common, Socrates says. "What is so wonderful [*thaumaston*] about that?" This word, "wonderful," comes from the same root of the word Plato uses when he says that philosophy begins *in wonder*. See *Theaetetus* 155c–d, where Theaetetus confesses that he is "lost in wonder" at Socrates' puzzles about being and becoming. Socrates answers, "The sense of wonder [*to thaumazein*, literally, "the wondering"] is the mark of the philosopher. Philosophy indeed has no other origin." Trans. Cornford, 1957, 43. See also *Meno* 84c: the slave boy only begins to inquire when he begins *to wonder*. The passages from *Meno* and *Theaetetus* may well be the source of Aristotle's remark that "philosophy begins in wonder" at *Metaphysics*, I, 982b.

22. See below, 53–8, on self-predication.

23. In this particular, I differ from most other scholars, who think that Socrates prefers the lump-of-gold analogy. I will try to show that this analogy is inadequate, and that Plato arguably recognizes this.

24. Socrates says at the conclusion of this section of text, "Why do we not say goodbye to songs and poems, and get back to what I first asked?" (347c). Many scholars take their cue from Socrates here. Beresford calls Socrates' analysis of the poem "pedantic." See Beresford, 2005, 150, n. 59. Vlastos calls the extended gloss of Simonides a "tongue-in-cheek digression;" 1991, 136. Guthrie dismisses the passage as "splendid entertainment, but hardly philosophy." See Guthrie, 1986, IV, 227. Crombie thinks the episode shows that "you can make a poem mean anything you like.... Reliance on poetry... is misguided." Crombie, 1963, v. I, 234. Grube finds it to be illustration of the way Socrates can "out-sophisticate the sophists." Grube, 1980, 220. Frede takes it to be part of a "major interruption" in the dialogue, an interruption that is irrelevant to its overall argument. Frede, 1992, xxvii. I try to identify some philosophically compelling points arising out of the "Ode" below, 58–60.

25. Kahn thinks along with Penner that this is exactly what Plato is thinking. See Kahn, 1976, 25.

26. Socrates surely would deny having knowledge of good and evil, but Plato obviously thinks Socrates is virtuous (though Plato's Socrates would surely deny *knowing* that he is).

27. 433b, as "doing one's own work." Reeve's translation, 2004, 119.

28. See Vlastos, 1983, 56; the phrase also appears in Vlastos, unpublished.

CHAPTER THREE

1. Vlastos, 1981, 52–9.

2. In his 1967, 454–5, Vlastos writes that sometimes, Plato's logic is "a little wobbly." I concur.

3. Note here how substantial this concession is. Protagoras had maintained the utter independence of the virtues one from another; now, he seeks merely to separate off courage from the rest.

4. Vlastos maintained that "the bravest man I ever knew would have flunked an elenctic examination on the nature of courage." Quoted by Woodruff, 1992, 101.

In the *Meno*, Socrates maintains that people who achieve great things without being terribly reflective—soldiers in battle, for example—are divine. They possess true opinions in a way "no different from . . . prophets and tellers of oracles, who under divine inspiration, utter many truths, but have no knowledge of what they are saying" (99c). According to this revised view, it seems that one could be brave without being wise.

Yet one can, evidently, be temperate by nature (*Charmides* 157–8?) is enough to make us brave. it is more stable, but behevioral ehavior that she believvws that some things are worse than d) and one can exhibit wisdom about what is genuinely to be feared without having done much moral philosophy. The brave solider shows by her behavior that she believes that some things are worse than death. Discursive wisdom is best, since it is more stable, but behaviorally manifested wisdom is enough to make us brave.

5. For better or worse, the Greek word for "courage," *andreia*, is derivative of *andr-*, the genitive root for *anēr*, *man*, in the sense of *adult male human being*. *Andreia* comes to *manliness*. For this reason, one occasionally finds Socrates saying, "Be a man and answer," (*Gorgias* 494d) or referring to the "manly virtue" [*andros aretē*—*Protagoras* 325a2]. (Curious, however, that *andreia* is a feminine noun!)

6. See 127–8, n. 6.

7. This would disturb everybody but Penner, since unity, according to him, comes to strict identity, but unity is not a thesis about what we mean when we speak about courage. According to Penner, it would be true that wisdom about desire is courage, though we would not say this.

8. Quoted by Woodruff, 1992, 101.

9. Guthrie, 1986, 223.

10. Also, at *Sophist* 251a, Plato maintains that motion and being can combine, but not so motion and rest. Some forms, he now sees, "interweave" and some do not.

11. Savan, 1964.

12. Vlastos, 1981, 237

13. For example, Adam and Adam, 1905, ix allege that Plato identifies the non-just with the unjust. Guthrie, 1975, v. IV, 226 and Grube, 1980, 220 maintain that Plato fails to distinguish between the "is" of identity and the "is" of predication, though, they grant, he does later correct this error at *Sophist* 255cd. Guthrie finds self-predication ridiculous; he writes "Men have the characteristic, but justice *is* the characteristic" (Guthrie, 1975, v. IV, 223, n.2; cf. 222). Grube claims that Plato fails to distinguish contradictories from contraries (Grube, 1980, 220). Plato later, Grube might have noted, patches this up in the *Philebus*. In that dialogue, Plato comes to see that the view that the good for humanity is the life of physical pleasure is only the contrary, not the contradictory, of the view that the life of mental pleasure is the good for humanity, so the two do not exclude each other. Because *Philebus* is late, Plato's

later logic might well have been sharpened by Aristotle. See Aristotle's *Categories* 10 for the distinction between contradictories and contraries. Brown seeks to excuse Plato for the "evident flaws" in his arguments, indicating that the dialogue is intended to be an "invitation to philosophy," rather than a settled expression of Plato's own views. See Brown, in Beresford, 2005, xvi.

14. *Hippias Major* 289ab and *Symposium* 211a.

15. This understanding of self-predication will be seen to owe much to Nehamas' classic paper on self-predication. As Nehamas reads the theory of forms, particular F's "do not *deserve*" the title of "F." We may say that pious particulars are only "sort-of pious." See Nehamas,1979, 101.

16. And surely, he is right about this. Dogs are animals and cats are animals, so they have the predicate "being animals" in common. But it does not follow that dogs are cats.

17. Plato also feels sympathy for Meno, I think, when Meno says that sometimes, he thinks the sophists teach virtue and sometimes, he does not (*Meno* 95c). Virtue can be learned but it cannot be (reliably) taught, and so it is not quite right to say either that the students of the sophists are taught virtue or that they do not learn it. Laches, too, says at one point, "I am really getting annoyed at being unable to express what I think . . . I still think I know what courage is, but I cannot understand how it has escaped me just now so that I cannot pin it down in words and say what it is" (*Laches* 194b). At *Charmides* 159a, however, Socrates maintains that, if someone really is temperate, that person will have "a sense of its presence, by way of which that person will form an opinion...of what sort [of thing] it is." This, I think, is what we should aim for—fully articulating what is present already inside us. But that it is elusive, I think, Plato grants, and I believe he feels some sympathy for Laches and, indeed, for Meno.

18. In *Philebus* and in *Sophist* Plato shows awareness of false dilemmas. See note 13.

19. There is almost universal agreement among scholars that the Simonides exegesis is a distraction. Socrates says at its conclusion, "Why do we not say goodbye to songs and poems, and get back to what I first asked?" (347c). Many scholars take their cue from Socrates here. Vlastos calls the extended gloss of Simonides a "tongue-in-cheek digression." See Vlastos, 1991, 136. Guthrie dismisses the passage as "splendid entertainment, but hardly philosophy." See Guthrie, 1986, IV, 227. Crombie thinks the episode shows that "you can make a poem mean anything you like. . . . Reliance on poetry . . . is misguided." See Crombie 1963, I, 234. Grube finds it to be illustration of the way Socrates can "out-sophisticate the sophists." See Grube, 1980, 220. Frede takes it to be part of a "major interruption" in the dialogue, an interruption that is irrelevant to its overall argument. See Frede, 1992, xxvii.

But the passage goes on for eight Stephanus pages, from 339 to 347, and, as already noted, it would be unlike Plato to engage in such a long digression without having *some* point in mind. The dismissal of songs and poems in the *Protagoras* may be ironic.

CHAPTER FOUR

1. Vlastos, 1981a, 237. Penner thinks Plato means just what he says—that courage *is* the whole of virtue.
2. As noted by Penner, in Benson, 1992, 171–3.
3. As observed by Brickhouse and Smith, 2000, 164.
4. Vlastos, 1981a, 233.
5. The other virtue are parts of virtue, but wisdom is "the greatest part" (329a). I take "greatest" here to mean "most important," not "largest."
6. Brickhouse and Smith also make this point. See their 1997, 316.
7. As noted by Brickhouse and Smith, 1994, 14, n. 21.
8. See chapter 2, n. 6 for Wakefield's criticism of the biconditionality view.
9. See my 1992 for the spark plug-engine analogy.
10. Penner, 1992, 165.
11. Penner, 1992, 164–5.
12. Penner, 1992, 165. Emphasis Penner's.
13. Penner, 1992, 165.
14. See 85 and 99.
15. See 39–40 and 43 n. 4.
16. See Leibniz on the identity of indiscernables as the criterion of identity, in Loemker, 1975, 308 and 700.
17. See Quine, 2004.
18. Everett and Fisher suggest that epistemologists should focus on the empirical question of how we use "justification" and its cognates, and they suggest that this could be revealed by a conducting a survey among native speakers. Whether or not Gettier cases are problematic is, on their account, strictly an empirical question. Everett and Fisher maintain that there is nothing more for epistemology to be *about*. See Everett and Fisher, 1994.
19. Concerning this passage, see my 2008, 31–2, 62–3 and 85.
20 See chapter 4 of my 2008. This also resolves Meno's paradox. We know virtue locally—so we are not blundering about blindly when we discuss it. But we do not know it globally, so we do not have a comprehensive understanding of what it is (at least *not yet*.) Meno had relied on "Either we know it or we do not know it," and Socrates seeks to loosen up this disjunction.
21. *Republic* 331cd.
22. Brickhouse and Smith, 2000, 167–168. See also their 1997.
23. Brickhouse and Smith, 1989, 253. They are seconded by Taylor, 1998, 67–8. He adds that he thinks the theory as expounded by Socrates is incoherent, as it represents virtue as being both exclusively good instrumentally and as being also intrinsically good. See Taylor, 1998, 68–9. *Pace* Taylor, however, at *Republic* II, 358a, Socrates says justice is the "highest" kind of good, one that is both instrumentally *and* intrinsically good. What is true here of justice is, it is likely, also true of virtue generally.
24. Brickhouse and Smith, 2000, 171.

25. We may even use this analogy to draw further distinctions between the virtues. *Squeezing* their analogy, Brickhouse and Smith observe that a distinction can be drawn between different kinds of coastal navigation, harbor from seacoast navigation, for example. Both kinds of navigation, say Brickhouse and Smith, can be construed as "parts" of coastal navigation. Similarly, we can distinguish piety as a "part" of justice and as a more specific version of a more generic virtue, justice (Brickhouse and Smith, 2000, 171). They are responding to Vlastos' criticism of their view put forward in 1994 (69–72); Vlastos thinks they do not pay proper attention to the *parts* of virtue. See Vlastos, 1981b. Brickhouse and Smith seem to me to be to be *cooking* their analogy here. Note that we feel uncomfortable about the situation; we speak of "'the parts' of justice;" the inverted commas *parade* our uncertainty here.

26. See Brickhouse and Smith, 1994, 70.

27. But see immediately below on *kinds of wisdom*.

28. Courage-in-behavior can exhibit an understanding of what is (and what is not) truly dreadful, with or without theoretical wisdom (about *dread*) accompanying it.

29. As already noted, Penner thinks Socrates does not endorse either parts of the face or parts of gold. I have argued already that Penner's view is inadequate, and I take Socrates to be committed to the view that virtue has parts (329a). Again, I think the issue for Socrates is not whether virtue has parts, but rather what *kinds of parts* it has. Virtue is a whole of parts, but it is unlike any other whole of parts—at least, it is unlike other wholes of parts that scholars have suggested. It is unlike the world, unlike the skill of triangulation, unlike genus and species, etc.

30. Brickhouse and Smith, 2000, 168.

31. Failure to account for the special nature of justice also plagues Aristotelian moral philosophy, I think. One can be miserly or one can be a spendthrift, and generosity may fairly be represented as a mean between the two; one can be a coward or one can be rash, and courage may be fairly be represented as a mean between the two. But one cannot, it seems, be overly just. Aristotle tries to minimize this embarrassment by claiming that the initial heart of justice is one of distributing goods (as a judge does—the judge can award too much or too little, or the right amount to a plaintiff), but his architectonic has become at this point a Procrustean bed, I think. Justice is living the right kind of human life, the righteous life, and it does seem to be special among the virtues. In *Republic*, Plato represents justice as a whole-centered virtue, as opposed to wisdom, temperance and courage, which are all of them part-centered.

32. To tie piety to justice, Brickhouse and Smith also suggest that piety is "the application of the knowledge of good and evil that aids the gods in benefitting others" (1997, 322). But Socrates flatly rejects, so far as I can see, the notion that what we do here below benefits the gods—as if the gods are sitting up on Olympus, saying "Keep the smoke coming"! See *Euthyphro* 12 ce.

33. In one, storms rotate clockwise, while in the other, they rotate counterclockwise.

34. Kremm (2009) distinguishes the analysis of the concept of virtue from the specification of the psychological state (the "disposition or tendency"—25). Virtue is one as a concept but many as a collection of psychological states. Virtue is one from one point of view, and many from another—like a marriage.

35. Penner maintains that this is *true*.

36. But see immediately below on *kinds* of wisdom. Socrates would say he doesn't know if he is virtuous until he knows what virtue is. But he may still exhibit courage-in-behavior, as he did at Delium.

37. Courage-*in-behavior* can exhibit an understanding of what is and what is not truly dreadful, with or without theoretical wisdom about dread accompanying it.

38. On *Republic's* showing, justice is whole-centered while the other virtues are part-centered: courage is properly the virtue pf the will, etc.

39. Justice seems to lack intentionality.

40. Socrates does not know if he is virtuous, but he may be virtuous, nonetheless. He exhibits virtue-in-behavior even in the absence of (what he would count as) wisdom.

41. Storms rotate clockwise in one hemisphere, but counterclockwise in the other.

CHAPTER FIVE

1. See Davidson, 1985 and Jenks, 2010.

2. Vlastos marks this imprecision. He writes, "I cannot recall its like in any of Plato's Socratic dialogues" (Vlastos, 1981a, 230, n. 22). He writes that "it suggests that Socrates is hunting for the right words and has not quite found them" (1981a, 230). (If I am right, there is a good reason why he has not found the right words.) Vlastos, meanwhile, takes Plato's lack of clarity in the *Protagoras* to be a consequence of the dialogue's being very early, before he had "mastered . . . logical vocabulary and technique" (1981a, 230 n.22).

3. Contrast Protagoras, the slick, articulate sophist, with Hippias, who, in *Hippias Major*, appears to be somewhat dumb. He "defines" "beauty" as "a beautiful girl." See *Hippias Major* 287e.

4. Socrates apparently wants to warn Hippocrates away from Protagoras. The dialogue ends, however, without a resolution of the issue of whether Hippocrates will become a disciple of Protagoras. Instead, it ends with Protagoras predicting that Socrates may become famous—as though this were what Socrates desires! Fame and notoriety are, however, what Protagoras promises to Athenians and they are what he himself values.

5. Vlastos says this of Socrates. See Vlastos, 1981a, 230.

6. As I have already indicated, I think that Protagoras (ironically) speaks for Plato here. The virtues are not many and separable, like marbles in a bag, but they are not exactly identical to one another, either. They are the same—only different. In his novel, *The Crying of Lot 49,* Thomas Pynchon represents a group of ideologues called the Thanatoids. Their thesis is that everything is like death—only different!

7. In my 2010.

8. He is supplanted by Strangers.

9. It is the elenchos, replete with the "say only what you really believe" requirement, though it is supplemented, as Davidson observes, by division and collection. See Davidson, 1985, 15.

10. If you fail to posit "the one" (i.e., if you don't have a theory of forms), Parmenides warns, you will "utterly destroy the power of thought and language" (*Parmenides* 135bc).

11. Miller and Allen both understand the mention of Socrates' youth in the *Parmenides* in this way. See Allen, 1998 and Miller, 1986.

12. Santas, in his classic paper on the Form of the Good (1983), maintains that the Form of the Good is specifically the Form of the Good by a double inference. Not only is each form the very best of its kind (particular beautiful things are beautiful from one point of view, but ugly from another, while the form of beauty is "beautiful to all and always"—*Hippias Major* 289ac), but the system of organization of the forms is also the best possible system. This makes it unique.

13. At 77e, Meno says virtue is having lots of gold and silver. Everybody, including Meno himself, knows this is wrong. It may be that wealth is what Meno himself really values. He may be thinking (confusedly), "What is virtue? —Virtue is admirable. What do I admire? —Wealth."

14. See the "discovery" passage of *Republic* 432. "For a long time now, justice has been rolling around our feet . . ."

15. His name, Menōn, means "remainder." He is the remainder left behind by famous people of the past—Gorgias, Homer, Hesiod and so on.

16. Many scholars take the claim to be ironic. See Lamb, 1924, 198–9, n. 1; Brown, in Beresford, 2005, xv; Guthrie, 1986, 227; and Frede, 1992, xxx.

17. Because this way of speaking seems perfectly acceptable to the Many, it appears that ordinary language considerations are inconclusive.

18. Note that Protagoras says at 349e that virtue is honorable, "unless I am quite mad." It may be both are true—virtue is honorable *and* Protagoras the subjectivist is quite mad.

19. Wittgenstein, 2001, § 261.

CHAPTER SIX

1. As, perhaps, the stuff in "irregular motion" that the demiurge has to work with is stubbornly resistant to form. The demiurge does the best he can with what he has to work with. Mohr is a bit more Manichaean than Plato; he writes that matter has a "certain cussedness." See Mohr, 1985, 4. Matter, I think, is not so much evil as it is independent—it has its own nature, which is why it must be "persuaded."

2. Kahn, 1976, 23 cites the passage to show that Plato continues to believe as late as *Laws* that there is unity *there* to be seen. I think it is also significant that unity is seen, i.e., not argued for, not even stated, but *seen*.

3. Note that Socrates and Meno come to this discovery about virtue without ever having defined "virtue." What Socrates says at the outset, viz., that he cannot say anything about virtue unless and until he knows what virtue is (71ab), is evidently false, and Plato evidently knows this. In the *Meno*, I think, we begin to see Plato turning away from the historical Socrates.

4. Santas' discussion of just what Socrates seeks in asking for definitions is quite useful. See Santas, 1979, 126–35.

5. Although he appeals to the story throughout his career, he argues for reincarnation only twice, once in *Meno* and once in *Phaedo*, and in both cases, he backs away from the argument immediately upon having given it. See my 2010, 77–9.

6. See Santas, 1983.

7. Santas in Anton and Preus, eds., 1983, 236. For the very useful distinction between formal and proper attributes, please see Keyt, 1969.

8. This is a thumbnail sketch of the argument I develop in my 2011.

9. Meno's Paradox asks, if I do not know that virtue is, how will I recognize it even if I stumble across it? See *Meno* 80d. The puzzle here is even deeper. If I am not sure what *giving an account* is, how can I give an account of it?

10. See my 2010, 133–7.

11. For suppose there were no such thing as truth. Then the sentence "There is no such thing as truth" would be true, in which case, there would be at least one true sentence. So "There is no such thing as truth" turns out to be one of those sentences which if true, is false. And if it is false, it is false, so I conclude that it's pretty much just false!

CHAPTER SEVEN

1. Actually, this is one of many that theses scholars refer to as "The Socratic Paradox." See Santas, 1979, 183–94; Irwin, 1977, 78–86. Vlastos thinks Socrates himself is a paradox. See Vlastos, 1980a in Vlastos, 1980b, 1–21.

2. See Brickhouse and Smith, 1994, 98. They write that knowing ourselves comes to "discovering who we are." See Brickhouse and Smith, 1994, 102.

3. Santas, 1979, 186–9 distinguishes between the actual object of desire and the intended object of desire (which is the Good). Brickhouse and Smith write that real benefit to himself is "what the tyrant really wanted all along." See Brickhouse and Smith, 1994, 90.

4. Compare to Augustine on time. He testifies that he has no trouble saying how much time an event took or what time an event is scheduled for, but when he asks himself in a philosophical tone of voice, *What is time?* his mind is a blank. See Augustine, *Confessions,* X, 1–16.

5. Press, 2001, 256 n. 13.

6. West and West, 1986, 3.

7. Of course, Socrates could be seeking to expose Charmides and Critias as frauds, but this kind of negative, aggressive use of the elenchos is one which Socrates rejects in *Apology*. The technique used just to humiliate an opponent, and not as a way of seeking the truth, is what Socrates' young followers are criticized for. See *Apology* 33c and ff.

8. I suspect that Plato is thinking here of the historical Socrates, who denied knowing what virtue is, but who succeeded in making Plato himself virtuous.

9. Brickhouse and Smith have a very useful discussion of the issue, 1994, 88–94. The thesis is the contrary of what we may call the Molly Bloom thesis. Molly Bloom thinks she must indulge her desires, for, otherwise, "What am I to do with all these desires?" (Joyce, 1961, 754). Plato thinks we are not just *stuck* with our desires.

10. Or perhaps babies are wise, via the recollection hypothesis of *Meno* and *Phaedo*. But this hypothesis can be read metaphorically: It is *as if* we had forgotten and are now being reminded of what we formerly knew. What we "recollect" has a feeling of familiarity to it. When we discover what justice is, we say, "Of Course! I knew that all along!" See the "discovery" passage at *Republic* 432e: justice has been "rolling around at our feet from the beginning, yet, like ridiculous fools, we could not see it." (Trans. Reeve, 2004, 118.) Concerning the line that recollection in *Meno* and *Phaedo* is intended metaphorically, see my 2010, ch. 4.

11. This presupposes Assumption 1.

12. This presupposes Assumption 2. Translation of this section of text is by Guthrie, 1956, 99.

13. Taking Socrates at his word that the phenomenon is rare. The other possibility is that everyone has a daimonion whispering in her ear, but that most people are hard of hearing.

14. Frede, 1992, x.

15. Kahn says the same about Socrates' argument against Gorgias. See Kahn, 1983, 119–20.

16. This is what Popper attributes to Plato. Popper's Plato says, "Here I am, your natural ruler. But I will not come begging." See Popper, 1962, 154–5. Popper's Plato evidently expects to be named ruler by acclamation.

17. Burnyeat, 1989 comes to this conclusion.

18. Polemarchus threatens, along with his friends, to pummel Socrates if he refuses to accompany them to his house. Socrates asks, "Isn't there another way? Can't I persuade you to let us go?" Polemarchus, fancying himself clever, replies, "How can you persuade us if we won't listen?" See *Republic* 327e. This actually is a profound question—How do you persuade people who won't listen? When the philosopher returns to the cave (517a ff.), he sits down with the prisoners and tells them stories. (One such story begins, "I went down to the Piraeus. . . .") Telling stories is one way to try to reach people who refuse instruction.

19. See my 2008, 56–66.

20. See Kahn, 1983, 78; Irwin, 1977, 116–7; and my 2007, 204–5.

21. Like Gorgias, Protagoras is also non-Athenian. He hails from Abdera in north-eastern Greece. He is made to express concern not to offend Athens, since he is a visitor: "A man has to be careful," says he, "when he visits powerful cities as a foreigner . . ." (316cd). He was eventually banished from Athens for impiety, since he was quite forthright about his agnosticism. As he departed, he was drowned owing to a shipwreck. See Guthrie, 1971, 263. Though his worry about expressing unpopular ideas was born out by his subsequent exile, I find no evidence that he is holding back in the *Protagoras* for political reasons.

22. Kahn, 1983, 83–4

23. See Kahn, 1983, 78, and Jenks, 2007

24. The distinction between moral and intellectual virtue is found in Aristotle, *NE*, VI.

25. Brickhouse and Smith challenge this piece of orthodoxy in their 2010.

26. Vlastos, as quoted by Woodruff, 1992, 101.

27. In their discussion of another issue, Brickhouse and Smith make this point. See Brickhouse and Smith, 1994, 92–3, n. 27.

28. Reeve, 1988, 114. The nuptial number is the number of years between Great Years, when all the planets and stars line up. The rarity of this sort of event represents cosmically the unlikelihood of all the elements coming together in just the right way. The heavenly bodies are "heavenly gods," and divine intervention is required to bring about kallipolis.

29. We might add here, "the honor, specially, of victory in argument." Timocrats and philosophers both argue, and both focus on abstract subjects, but they are differently motivated.

30. Cornford, 1997, 165.

31. See my 2002 and Erhardt, 1986.

32. See also Brickhouse and Smith, 1989, 237–57 and 1994, 189–95.

33. Grube's representation of the line seems to me both clear and consistent with the text. See Grube, 1974, 164.

34. Annas takes the different lengths of the line segments to reflect different levels of clarity in the various proper objects of the epistemic functions. But she does not explain their precise mathematical relations. See Annas in Kraut, 1997, 148–9. Cornford says shorter segments have lower degrees of "reality and truth," (Cornford, 1945, 221), but he also does not account for Plato's precision.

35. See Cornford, 1945, 269, n. 3.

36. Reeve concurs. See Reeve, 1988, 114.

37. See Dodds, 1990, 11.

38. I think Plato is challenging us. "You must go down. How will you choose to go down?"

39. DL 3.5; see also Guthrie, v. IV, 1975, 12–3.

40. It is my sense of things that the *Phaedrus*, nominally about love, is really about love of discourse. See also Griswold, 1986, 161.

41. See Reeve's useful discussion, 1988, 238–41.

42. See also Dodd's classic study, 1951, 183–8. Brickhouse and Smith also cite several extra-rational sources of illumination—dreams, oracles, and the like. See Brickhouse and Smith, 1989, 237–57 and 1994, 189–95. For the opposing point of view, see Vlastos, who seeks to analyze away Socrates' apparent reliance on such sources. See Vlastos, 1991, 280–7.

43. See especially *Meno* 78a, 88c and 89ac. See also, *Gorgias* 199d.

44. Woodruff, 1976, and Brickhouse and Smith, 1997; see also Kremm, who argues that, even without knowing all good and evil, one can still exhibit "virtuous output." See Kremm, 2009, 26.

45. Vlastos, "The Paradox of Socrates," in Vlastos, ed., 1971, 4.

46. He does this again at *Meno* 86c. Meno is ready to throw in the towel, to abandon all inquiry. Socrates prods him, asserting that "we will be better, braver and

less slothful if we continue to inquire . . ." Note the suggestion that Meno's primary problem is that he is lazy.

47. See *Theaetetus* 165b. See also my 2008.

48. An understanding of some of the virtues, although, I think, not of all of them. The gods can be praised for their kindness or generosity (they send the daimonion to Socrates, for example) and for their justice, but, since they need not fear death, it is hard to see how the gods can be courageous.

CHAPTER EIGHT

1. This, at any rate, is the way Plato himself construes Xeno's argument. See *Parmenides* 126a. A different construal is to take Xeno as a trickster: his arguments weigh equally against Parmenides *and* his critics. See Miller, 1991, 5.

2. He says at *Sophist* 217c8–9 that he was very young when the (alleged) conversation took place Parmenides was born between 515 and 510 BCE, while Socrates was born in 470 BCE. If their alleged conversation took place in 451 BCE, Socrates would have been 19. The dates I reference here are from Guthrie, 1971, 58 and 1975, v. II, 1–2.

3. Allen, 1983; Miller, 1986

4. I think this passage can safely be de-mythologized, to borrow Tillich's phrase. See Tavard, 1962, 4. We are blessed with true beliefs, beliefs we have not *earned*. Following out the traces of such beliefs, we arrive at the truth that had previously eluded us. So, whether or not the truth of true beliefs demonstrably comes from the gods, it is *as if* such beliefs are gifts from the gods.

5. *Meno* features a few instances in which Plato plays a bit fast and loose with metaphor. Unveiling an insight is *like* succeeding in recollecting something we had previously forgotten (it has a kind of *familiarity*), but Plato writes as if we really are recollecting things learned in previous lifetimes (85de). It is *as if* unreflective but admirable persons are divinely inspired, but Plato writes as though such people really *are* divine (99c). The statues of Daedalus are so lifelike that they *seem* to move, but Plato writes as if they really are in danger of moving away and so need to be chained down (97d–98a). In 2011, 105, I seek to explain Plato's treating metaphors as literal assertions here in *Meno*.

6. This may appear to be inconsistent with the re-incarnation story, according to which we learned (sc. what virtue is) in a former lifetime. However, as Nehamas observes, the requisite abilities have *always* been in the soul (85d), i.e., there was no initial learning. See Nehamas, 1985, 30.

7. Vlastos, 1983, 46.

8. I concede that in the *Laches*, Plato objects to the claim that courage is wisdom about past, present and future good and evil by observing that this characterizes *all* of virtue (not just that part of virtue we call "courage"). But I do not take "wisdom about all good and evil" to be offered as a *definition* of "virtue-in-general." To cite a parallel case, it is true that virtue is a benefit to the virtuous person, but "what is beneficial to the virtuous person" is not offered as a definition of "virtue." "Involving wisdom

about what is good and bad for us," like "being beneficial to us," is a true predicate of "virtue," but it is not, and it is not offered as, a definition of "virtue."

9. Keith McPartland suggested this case at a conference on the unity of the virtues held at Oregon State University, April, 2005.

10. Penner would dismiss this point, since the unity thesis, on his showing, has nothing to do with words or their meaning, but I think the point is instructive. Clark, 2015, meanwhile, thinks that the virtues are one psychologically but many conceptually, both like the parts of a face and like the "parts" of gold. I have given reasons for being dissatisfied with both analogies.

I believe that there are certain natural tendencies—tendencies given to us by nature—which, if indulged to the fullest, would make collective, civilized life impossible. We have a natural tendency to flee in the face of danger. Courage is the principled resistance of that natural tendency. We have a natural tendency to cling to our own possessions. Generosity is the principled resistance to that natural tendency. We have a natural propensity to behave—pardon my French!—like assholes. Justice is the principled resistance to that natural tendency. And so on. If this sort of account can be maintained in the case of all the virtues, it will emerge that virtue is uniquely civilizing. We are by nature social beings, and virtue *enables* collective, social life. See also McPherran, 2000, on *Republic*'s complex "internalist" moral psychology.

11. In *Apology*, his name is mentioned as one of Socrates' associates who have agreed to pony up a fine, should the jury decide on that as a punishment. In *Phaedo*, it is intimated that Plato was not present when Socrates was executed. See *Apology* 38b and *Phaedo* 59b. Plato is also referred to at *Apology* 34a, as one who engaged in "discussions" with Socrates.

12. "Platōn," like our English word "plateau," refers to any broad, flat expanse of territory. Scholars have speculated on why Plato was so named (or so nick-named). Santas thinks it is because Plato was over-weight—hence, he is "broad." Lee thinks it is because Plato had a noticeably wide forehead, so that "Plato" came to something like "Mr. Broad Forehead." His given name was Aristocles, according to Alexander of Miletus, quoted by Diogenes Laertius, "Life of Plato," 1925, v. I, 4.

CHAPTER NINE

1. And what justifies the super-principle? Mill says the Greatest Happiness Principle cannot be grounded in anything else, since it is the ground of everything. See Mill, in Sher, 2001, 38. Kant represents the Categorical Imperative as the condition of rationality; the immoral person is fundamentally *confused*. See Kant, in Beck, 1990, 18–9.

2. It does seem a bit peculiar that the obvious and plausible option that ethics is complicated does not seem to arise. Why not say that being a good person is partly having a good character and partly also operating according to the right principles? I am reminded of Austin's remark that it is not things but philosophers that are simple. See Austin, 1964, 4.

3. The right thing is not just what we desire since we often desire bad things. The right thing is, rather, what we desire to desire. See Ross, 2002, 16–8.

4. At the outset of *The Wasteland*, Eliot quotes Petronius *Satiricon* 48.8: "For I saw with my own eyes the celebrated Sibyl at Cumae. And when the acolyte said, 'What is it that you wish, o Sibyl?' she replied, 'I wish to die.'"

5. He needs to be able to represent being-a-good-person without recourse to principles of action. He does so, as do other virtue theorists, by positing a moral hero.

6. See Vlastos, 1980, 6–7.

7. His name means "remainder," "that which remains." He is the remainder left behind by famous people in the past—Homer, Hesiod, Pindar, Gorgias, etc.

8. In striving to make room for Plato's view, I try to show that it is not just consistent with but also strongly suggested by things he says about virtue elsewhere. But I also in some sense *agree* with the view I attribute to him. I am attracted by virtue theory, and so I, too, think the virtues must be unified, and for the same reason I attribute to Plato: it must be possible, *sans* resort to principles, to live a fully virtuous life. But how virtue can be one *and* many is beyond me, and, as I indicate here, quite possibly beyond everybody. However, in attributing to Plato a view I myself find congenial, I do not think I am alone. I think Penner himself thinks the virtues really are identical and that Brickhouse and Smith themselves think the virtues really are applications of the same skill in different contexts.

9. Christians say that, as you approach the gate of heaven, above the entrance, you will see the words "Enter, all ye who would." After you go through the gate and turn around to look at the back side of the gate, you will see the words "Chosen before the foundation of the world." Christians say that both are true—we freely enter into what we are predestined for. Of course, we don't understand this. Augustine writes, *Credo ut intelligum*: he "believes [now] in order that he might understand [later]" (Burt, 1996, 45), and St. Paul writes that "now we see as through a glass darkly, but later, face to face" (Corinthians 13,12). Writers other than Plato have thought that there are truths that are beyond our capacity to apprehend or even to properly *state*. One could, I suppose, hold that the virtues are one and many in the way that God is three persons and one God, but this would be *obscurum per obscurius*.

10. Rudebusch, 2017, 338

11. Rudebusch, 2017, 343

12. In striving to make room for Plato's view, I try to show that it is not just consistent with but also strongly suggested by things he says about virtue elsewhere. But I also in some sense agree with the view I attribute to him. I myself am attracted by virtue theory, and I, too, think that the virtues must be unified, and for the same reason I attribute to Plato: it must be possible, *sans* resort to principles of action (commandments and the like), to live a fully virtuous life, but how exactly, virtue can be both one and many is beyond me, and, as I indicate here, quite possibly beyond *everybody*. But in attributing to Plato a view I myself find congenial; I do not think I am alone. I think that Penner himself thinks the virtues really are identical and that Brickhouse and Smith themselves think the virtues really are applications of the same skill in different contexts.

13. Christians say that, as you approach the gates of heaven, you will see written on one side the words "Enter all ye who would." As you pass through, you can turn around and see written on the other side the words "Chosen before the foundation of the world." Christians say that both are true—we freely enter into what we are predestined for. Of course, we don't currently understand this. Augustine writes *Credo ut intelligum*—"I believe [now] in order that I might understand [later]." (Burt, 1996, 45). Concerning the Incarnation, Paul writes, "Now we see as through a glass darkly, but later, face to face" (Corinthians 13,12). There are truths that are beyond our capacity to apprehend or even properly to state. One could, I suppose, hold that the virtues are both one and many in the way that God is three persons in one, but this would be *obscurum par obscurius*.

CONCLUSION

1. Allen, 1970, 94–5. See also Yonezawa, 2012, who offers a similar understanding.
2. See Clark, 2015.
3. Wisdom, 1970, 138.

Bibliography

Adam, J., and A. M. Adam, eds. *Plato*, Protagoras, *2nd Edition*. New York and Cambridge: Cambridge University Press, 1905.
Allen, R. E. *Plato's* Euthyphro *and the Earlier Theory of Forms*. London and New York: Routledge and Kegan Paul, 1970.
Allen, Reginald E. *Plato's* Parmenides: *Translation and Analysis*. New Haven and London: Yale University Press, 1998.
Apolloni, David. *The Self-Predication Assumption in Plato*. Lanham: Lexington Books, 2011.
Aristotle. *Nicomachean Ethics*. Translated by Robert C. Bartlett and Susan D. Collins. Chicago and London: University of Chicago Press, 2011.
Aristotle. *The Organon, Complete Edition*. Translated by Octavius Freire Owen,
Austin, J. L. *Philosophical Papers, 2nd Edition*. Edited by J. O. Urmson and G. J. Warnock. New York and Oxford: Oxford University Press, 1970.
Austin, J. L. *Sense and Sensibilia, Reconstructed from Manuscript Notes by G. J. Warnock*. New York: Galaxy, Oxford University Press, 1964.
Beck, Lewis White, trans. *Immanuel Kant: Foundations of the Meta-physics of Morals*. Upper Saddle River: Prentice-Hall, 1990.
Benson, Hugh H., ed. *Essays on the Philosophy of Socrates*. New York and Oxford: Oxford University Press, 1992.
Beresford, Adam, trans. *Plato:* Protagoras *and* Meno, *with an Introduction by Lesley Brown*. London: Penguin, 2005.
Bianco, Lino. "The Unity of Courage and Wisdom in Plato's *Protagoras*," *Philosophia* 11 (2016): 5–13.
Bloom, Allan, trans. *The Republic of Plato, 2nd Edition*. New York: Basic Books, 1991.
Bloomfield, Paul, ed. *Morality and Self-Interest*. New York and Oxford: Oxford University Press, 2008.
Brickhouse Thomas C., and Nicholas D. Smith. "Socrates and the Unity of the Virtues." *Journal of Ethics* 1 (1997): 311–24.

Brickhouse, Thomas C., and Nicholas D. Smith. *Socrates on Trial.* Princeton: Princeton University Press, 1989.

Brickhouse Thomas C., and Nicholas D. Smith. *Socratic Moral Psychology.* New York: Cambridge University Press, 2010.

Brickhouse Thomas C., and Nicholas D. Smith. *The Philosophy of Smith, Socrates.* Boulder: Westview Press, 2000.

Brown, Lesley. "Introduction" to *Plato:* Protagoras *and* Meno, *with an Introduction by Lesley Brown,* translated by Adam Beresford. London: Penguin, 2005.

Burt, Donald X. *Augustine's World: An Introduction to His Speculative Philosophy.* London: University Press of America, 1996.

Cahn, Steven M. *Exploring Ethics: An Introductory Anthology.* Oxford and New York: Oxford University Press, 2009.

Clark, Justin C. "Socrates, the Primary Question and the Unity of Virtue." *Canadian Journal of Philosophy* 45 (2015): 445–70.

Cooper, John. "The Unity of Virtue." In *Reason and Emotion: Essays on Ancient Moral Psychology.* Princeton: Princeton University Press, 1999.

Crombie, I. M. *An Examination of Plato's Doctrines, Volumes 1 and 2.* New York: Humanities Press, 1962–3.

Davidson, Donald. "Plato's Philosopher." *London Review of Books* 7, no. 14 (1985): 15–7. In *Meditations on First Philosophy,* by Haldane and Ross, 1931.

Devereux, Daniel. "Socrates' Kantian Conception of Virtue." *Journal of the History of Philosophy* 33, 381–408.

Dodds, E. R. *The Greeks and the Irrational.* Berkeley and Los Angeles: University of California Press, 1951.

Ehrhardt, Edit. "The Word of the Muses Plato, Rep. 8.546." *Classical Quarterly* 80, no. 26 of the Continuous Series (1986): 407–420.

Eno, Robert. *The Analects of Confucius, An Online Teaching Translation.* www.indiana.edu/~p374 Eno-2015.pdf.

Everson, Stephen, ed. *Companions to Ancient Thought 1: Epistemology.* Cambridge and New York: Cambridge University Press, 1990.

Falk, W. D. "Morality, Self and Others." In *Morality and Self-*Interest, edited by Paul Bloomfield, 205–250. New York and Oxford: Oxford University Press, 2008.

Ferejohn, Michael. "Socratic Virtue as the Parts of Itself." *Philosophy and Phenomenological Research* 44 (1984): 377–88.

Fisher, Alec, and Nicholas Everitt. *Modern Epistemology: A New Introduction.* New York: McGraw-Hill, 1994.

Frede, Michael. "Introduction." In *Plato:* Protagoras, edited and translated by S. Lombardo and K. Bell, vii–xxxiv. Indianapolis and Cambridge: Hackett, 1992.

Freud, Sigmund. *Three Case Histories,* kindle edition. Edited by Philip Rieff,. New York: Simon and Schuster, 1963.

Friedlander, Paul. *Plato: An Introduction.* Princeton: Princeton University Press, 1958.

Futter, Dylan. "Nicias Fights in Armour: Sophistical Self-Defence in Plato's *Laches*," unpublished.

Gallop, David. "The Socratic Paradox in the *Protagoras*." *Phronesis* 9 (1964): 117–29.

Gerson, Lloyd. Review of Apoloni, 2011. In *Bryn Mawr Classical Review*. 2012.

Griswold, Charles L. "Philosophy, Education, and Courage in Plato's *Laches*." *Interpretation* 14 (1986): 177–193.

Griswold, Charles L. *Plato's* Phaedrus. New Haven: Yale University Press, 1986.

Grube, G. M. A. *Plato's Thought*. Indianapolis and Cambridge: Hackett, 1980.

Guthrie, W. K. C. "*Protagoras, Meno, Euthydemus, Gorgias, Menexenus*." In *A History of Greek Philosophy, IV. Plato, The Man and His Dialogues: Earlier Period*. Cambridge and New York: Cambridge University Press, 1975.

Guthrie, W. K. C., ed. and trans. *Plato:* Protagoras *and* Meno. London and New York: Penguin, 1956.

Haldane, Elizabeth S., and G. R. T. Ross, eds. and trans. *The Philosophical Works of Descartes, volumes 1 and 2*. London: Cambridge University Press, 1931.

Irwin, Terence. *Plato's Moral Theory: The Early and Middle Dialogues*. New York and Oxford: Oxford University Press, 1977.

Irwin, Terrence. *Plato's Moral Theory: The Early and Middle Dialogues*. Oxford: Clarendon Press, 1977.

Irwin, Terence. "The *Protagoras*." In *Plato's Ethics*. New York and Oxford: Oxford University Press, 1995.

Jenks, Rod. *How Plato's Theory of Truth Explains Socratic Method*. Lewiston and Lampeter: Edwin Mellen Press, 2010.

Jenks, Rod. *Plato on Moral Expertise*. Lanham: Lexington, 2008.

Jenks, Rod. "Socratic Piety and Socrates' Defense." *The Modern Schoolman* 82 (2005): 193–210.

Jenks, Rod. "The Machinery of the Collapse: On *Republic* VIII." *History of Political Thought* 23 (2002): 21–9.

Kahn, Charles H. "Drama and Dialectic in Plato's *Gorgias*." *Oxford Studies in Ancient Philosophy* I (1983): 75–121.

Kahn, Charles H. "Plato on the Unity of the Virtues." In Werkemeister, 1976, 21–39

Kitching, Gavin N. "Resolutely Ethical: The Dogmatism of Analysis and Contemporary Wittgenstein Scholarship." In *Wittgenstein and Society: Essays in Conceptual Puzzlement*, 179–222. Aldershot and Burlington: Ashgate, 2003.

Kraut, Richard. *Socrates and the State*. Princeton: Princeton University Press, 1984.

Kremm, Douglas. "The Unity of Virtue: Toward a Middle Ground Between Identity and Inseparability in Socratic Virtue." *Arche* 3 (2009): 15–30.

Lee, E. N., A. P. D. Mourelatos, and R. M. Rorty, eds. *Exegesis and Argument: Studies in Greek Philosophy Presented to Gregory Vlastos, Phronesis* Supplementary Volume I. New York: Humanities Press, 1973.

Loeb, ed. *Plato II:* Laches, Protagoras, Meno, Euthydemus. Translated by W. R. M. Lamb. Cambridge and London: Harvard University Press, 1924.

Lombardo, S., and K. Bell, eds. and trans. *Plato:* Protagoras. Indianapolis and Cambridge: Hackett, 1992.

Malcolm, John. *Plato on the Self-Predication of Forms: Early and Middle Dialogues*. Oxford: Clarendon Press, 1991.

McDowell, John, trans. *Plato:* Theaetetus, *Translated with Notes by John McDowell.* New York and Oxford: Oxford University Press, 1973.

McDowell, John, trans. *Plato:* Theaetetus, *With an Introduction and Notes by Lesley Brown.* New York and Oxford: Oxford University Press, 2014.

McPherran, Mark. "Piety, Justice and the Unity of the Virtues." *Journal of the History of Philosophy* 38 (2000): 299–328.

Meinwald, Constance C. "Good-bye to the Third Man." In *The Cambridge Companion to Plato*, edited by Richard Kraut. Cambridge and New York: Cambridge University Press, 1992.

Mencius. *Mencius, An Online Teaching Translation.* Translated by Robert Eno. www.indiana.edu/~374/Mengzi.pdf, 2016.

Miller, Mitchell H. *Plato's* Parmenides: *The Conversion of the Soul.* Princeton: Princeton University Press, 1986.

Mohr, Richard. *The Platonic Cosmology.* Leiden: E. J. Brill, 1985.

Nehamas, Alexander. "Self-Predication and Plato's Theory of Forms." *American Philosophical Quarterly* 16 (1979).

Penner, Terry. "Socrates on the Strength of Knowledge: *Protagoras* 351B–357E." *Archiv für Geschichte der Philosophie* 29 (1997): 117–49.

Penner, Terry. "The Unity of Virtue." *Philosophical Review* 35 (1973). In *Essays on the Philosophy of Socrates*, edited by Hugh H. Benson, 162–84. New York and Oxford: Oxford University Press, 1992.

Press, Gerald A. "The Elenchos in Plato's *Charmides*, 162–75." In *Does Socrates Have a Method? Rethinking the Elenchus in Plato's Dialogues and Beyond*, edited by Gary Alan Scott, 252-65. University Park: Pennsylvania State University Press, 2001.

Pynchon, Thomas. *The Crying of Lot 49.* Philadelphia: J. B. Lippincott, 1966.

Quine, W. V. O. *"Epistemology Naturalized."* In *Epistemology: An Anthology*, edited by E. Sosa and J. Kim, 292–300. Malden: Blackwell Publishing, 2004.

Rayan, Sobhi. "Unity of Virtues According to Socrates and Protagoras." *International Journal of Philosophy and Theology* 2 (2014): 151–63.

Rickless, Samuel L. "Socrates' Moral Intellectualism." *Pacific Philosophical Quarterly* 79 (1998): 355–67.

Robinson, Richard. "Elenchus." In *Plato: A Collection of Critical Essays, I: Metaphysics and Epistemology*, edited by Gregory Vlastos, 78–93. Notre Dame: University of Notre Dame Press, 1971.

Rohlf, Michael. "Immanuel Kant." *Stanford Encyclopedia of Philosophy* 5 (2018): 114–24.

Rorty, Richard. *Philosophy and the Mirror of Nature.* Princeton: Princeton University Press, 1980.

Ross, W. D. *The Right and the Good.* Edited by Philip Stratton-Lake. Oxford: Clarendon Press, 2002.

Rudebusch, George. "The Unity of Virtue, Ambiguity and Socrates' Higher Purpose." *Ancient Philosophy* 37 (2017): 333–46.

Rutherford, Richard. "Unifying the *Protagoras*." *Apeiron* 25 (1992): 133–56.

Saint Augustine. *Essential Sermons*, Introduction and Notes by Daniel E. Doyle. Edited by Boniface Ramsey and translated by Edmund Hill. Hyde Park: New City Press, 2007.

Santas, Gerasimos. "Plato's *Protagoras* and Explanations of Weakness." *Philosophical Review* 75 (1966). In *The Philosophy of Socrates: A Collection of Critical Essays*, edited by Gregory Vlastos, 264–98. Notre Dame: University of Notre Dame Press, 1971.

Santas, Gerasimos Xenophon. "The Form of the Good in Plato's *Republic*." In *Essays in Ancient Greek Philosophy*, edited by John P. Anton and Anthony Preuss, 232–63. Albany: State University of New York Press, 1983.

Santas, Gerasimos Xenophon. "The Moral Paradox." In *Socrates: Philosophy in Plato's Early Dialogues*, 189-94. Boston and London: Routledge and Kegan Paul, 1979.

Scott, Gary Alan, ed. *Does Socrates Have a Method? Rethinking the Elenchus in Plato's Dialogues and Beyond*. University Park: Pennsylvania State University Press, 2001.

Sher, George, ed. *John Stuart Mill, Utilitarianism*. Indianapolis and Cambridge: Hackett, 2001.

Singer, Peter. "Famine, Affluence and Morality." *Philosophy and Public Affairs* 32 (1972). In *Exploring Ethics: An Introductory Anthology*, by Steven M. Cahn, 226–39. Oxford and New York: Oxford University Press, 2009.

Sprague, Rosamond K. *Plato's Use of Fallacy: A Study of the* Euthydemus *and Some Other Dialogues*. London: Routledge and Kegan Paul, 1962.

Strawson, P. F. "Truth." *Proceedings of the Aristotelian Society*, S.V. 24 (1950). In *Truth*, edited by George Pitcher. Englewood Cliffs: Prentice-Hall, 1964.

Sullivan, J. P. "The Hedonism in Plato's *Protagoras*." *Phronesis* 6 (1961): 10–28.

Tavard, George H. *Paul Tillich and the Christian Message*. London: Burns and Oates, 1962.

Thayer, H. S. "Plato's Quarrel with Poetry: Simonides." *Journal of the History of Ideas* 36 (1975): 3–26.

Vlastos, Gregory. "A Note on 'Pauline Predications' in Plato." *Phronesis* 19 (1874). In *Platonic Studies*, by Gregory Vlastos, 404-9. Princeton: Princeton University Press, 1981(a).

Vlastos, Gregory, ed. *The Philosophy of Socrates: A Collection of Critical Essays*. Notre Dame: University of Notre Dame Press, 1971.

Vlastos, Gregory. "Introduction." In *Plato's* Protagoras, translated by Benjamin Jowett and revised by Martin Ostwald. Indianapolis: Bobbs-Merrill, 1956.

Vlastos, Gregory. *Platonic Studies*. Princeton: Princeton University Press, 1981a.

Vlastos, Gregory. *Socrates, Ironist and Moral Philosopher*. Ithaca: Cornell University Press, 1991.

Vlastos, Gregory. "Socrates on *Akrasia*." *Phoenix* 23 (1969): 71–88.

Vlastos, Gregory. "Socrates on 'The Parts of Virtue.'" In Vlastos, 1981b, 418–23.

Vlastos, Gregory. "Socratic Perplexity: *Laches* 198a-199e." Referenced in "Socratic Virtue as the Parts of Itself," by Michael Ferejohn, 386, n. 21. *Philosophy and Phenomenological Research* 44 (1984): 377–88.

Vlastos, Gregory. "The Paradox of Socrates." *Queen's Quarterly* (1958). In *The Philosophy of Socrates: A Collection of Critical Essays*, edited by Gregory Vlastos. Notre Dame: Notre Dame University Press, 1980.

Vlastos, Gregory. "The Unity of the Virtues in the *Protagoras*." *Review of Metaphysics* 25 (1972). In *Platonic Studies*, by Gregory Vlastos, 221–69. Princeton: Princeton University Press, 1981(a).

Vlastos, Gregory. "Was Polus Refuted?" *American Journal of Philology* 88 (1967): 454–60.

Weiss, Roslyn. *The Socratic Paradox and its Enemies*. Chicago and London: University of Chicago Press, 2006.

Werkmeister, W. H., ed. *Facets of Plato's Philosophy*. Assen: Van Gorcum, 1976.

Wisdom, John. "Paradox and Discovery." *The Howison Lecture*. Berkeley, 1957. In *Paradox and Discovery*, 114–38. Berkeley and Los Angeles: University of California Press, 1970.

Wittgenstein, Ludwig. *Philosophical Investigations, 4th Edition*. Translated by G. E. M. Anscombe, P. M. S. Hacker and Joachim Schulte. Hoboken: Wiley-Blackwell, 2001.

Wolfsdorf, David. "Courage and Knowledge at *Protagoras* 349e-351b." *Classical Quarterly* NS 56 (2006): 436–44.

Wolfsdorf, David. "*Dunamis* in *Laches*." *Phoenix* 9 (2005): 324–47.

Woodruff, Paul. "Plato's Early Theory of Knowledge." In *Companions to Ancient Thought 1: Epistemology*, edited by Stephen Everson, 60-84. Cambridge and New York: Cambridge University Press, 1990.

Woodruff, Paul. "Socrates on the Parts of Virtue." *Canadian Journal of Philosophy* 6, Supplemental Volume I (1977): 101–16.

Index Locorum

Apology	19–20	78
	21b	6, 9
	21d	47
	23b	79
Charnides	155de	74
	157–8	38
	159a	54
	159c	55
	161	2
	165b	9
Cratylus	403–4	77
	427	53
	436ab	53
	439–40	53
	432–3	53
	463b	19
Euthyphro	4b	19
	6bc	79
	9d	55
	12	23, 76
Gorgias	331b	33
	331e	33
	331–2	33
	346–7	34
	449c	78
	467e	30
	470b	36
	473b	36
	473de	51

	477b	36
	509a	9
Hippias Major	289ac	1, 11
	289b	31
	289de	31
Laches	181b	36
	181–2	2
	186bc	78
	186de	36
	190	54
	190e	29
	191de	73, 76
	192a	4
	197e	78
	199ed	3
	198d	2
	191de	2, 3
	208	78
Laws	865d	42
	964ab	42
	965a	55
	965c	54
	965cd	54
	965b	54
Meno	71a	78
	71b	54
	71c	78
	73a	55
	73d	55
	76a	43
	77de	36
	78c	55
	78d	55
	81d	39
	86bc	50, 72
	86c	54
	86cd	54
	93a	54
	95bc	72
	96d	72
	97b	72
	98e	51
	99de	72
Parmenides	135bc	71
Phaedo	69–72	28
	74bc	31

Index Locorum 117

Phaedrus	274–9	56
Philebus	16b	49
Protagoras	311	48
	316a	47
	316d	48
	317bc	48
	3127c	48
	318b	18
	320-8	47
	323a	20
	324a	20
	324	20
	324-5	48
	327a	18
	328c	78
	330a	4
	330a	21–3, 24
	330b	22
	331a	22
	331ab	48
	331c	4, 48
	331d	48
	331e	7, 48, 73
	331–2	81
	332	22, 27, 30
	333b	48
	336cd	50
	342e	50
	344b	50–1
	345e	51
	348a	55
	348c	11, 81
	349d	28
	349e	28
	350c	24, 44
	359e	51
	353	29
	352–8	41
	357d	29
	358d	51
Republic	332a	3
	357a	4, 11
	357c	4, 8
	388a	8
	428b	54
	429c	54

	431–2	54
	432–3	4
	434–5	54
	479bc	32–3
	471e	76
	506 c	56
	509b	2
	534e	3
	540	55
	543e	1, 74
	596b	10
	599b	10
Theaetetus	177b	1
	196e	40
	206d	56

About the Author

Rod Jenks obtained a bachelor's degree in Philosophy, University of California, Berkeley, a bachelor's Degree in English, University of Oregon, and his PhD in Philosophy, University of California, San Diego. Jenks is currently teaching at the University of Portland. He has published various papers on Plato as well as three important books: *How Plato's Theory of Truth Explains Socratic Method: Consistency is the Test of Truth* (Lewiston: Edwin Mellen Press, 2010), *Plato on Moral Expertise* (Lanham: Lexington, 2008), and *How the Images in Plato's Dialogues Develop a Life of Their Own: When His Poetry Trumps His Philosophy* (Lewiston: Edwin Mellen Press, 2011).

www.ingramcontent.com/pod-product-compliance
Lightning Source LLC
Chambersburg PA
CBHW061719300426
44115CB00014B/2758